D1346531

AMAZING FANTASTIC INCREDIBLE

A **MARVELOUS** MEMOIR

STAN LEE

and PETER DAVID
and COLLEEN DORAN

SIMON & SCHUSTER
London New York Toronto Sydney New Delhi

CONTRIBUTORS

Written by

STAN LEE and PETER DAVID
with contributions from POW! Entertainment

Art by

COLLEEN DORAN

Colors by
BILL FARMER
with Val Trullinger, Juan Fernandez, Joseph Baker, and Jose Villarubia

Letterer, Classic Comics Restoration, and Research Assistant
ALLAN HARVEY

Background Art Assistant
RANTZ HOSELEY

The art team on this project, with all humility and respect, acknowledges our debt to the creators who came before us and whose work helped make this book.

With most sincere thanks to:

Joe Maneely	Larry Lieber	John Romita, Sr.	Barry Windsor-Smith
Steve Ditko	Joe Simon	Jim Steranko	John Buscema
Adam Hughes	Arnold Sawyer	Frank Kelly Freas	Charles Addams
Gil Kane	Alex Saviuk	Scott McDaniel	Klaus Janson
Syd Shores	Frank R. Paul	Sol Brodsky	George Tuska
Mike Esposito	Frank Giacoia	Vince Colletta	John Carter
John Severin	Wally Wood	Alan Weiss	Gray Morrow
Don Heck	Dick Ayers	George Klein	Joe Sinnott
Irving Forbush (just because)		and especially our king, Jack Kirby	

The Marvel and DC Comics logos appear courtesy of and are registered trademarks of Marvel Entertainment and DC Comics.

We also wish to thank those who contributed additional photo references. These were used courtesy of:

Max Anderson   Michael Uslan   Gerry Conway   Joe Field and Flying Colors   Spencer Beck

The art team has donated a portion of the proceeds for this book to the Hero Initiative, an organization dedicated to supporting cartoonists in need. Learn more at www.heroinitiative.org.

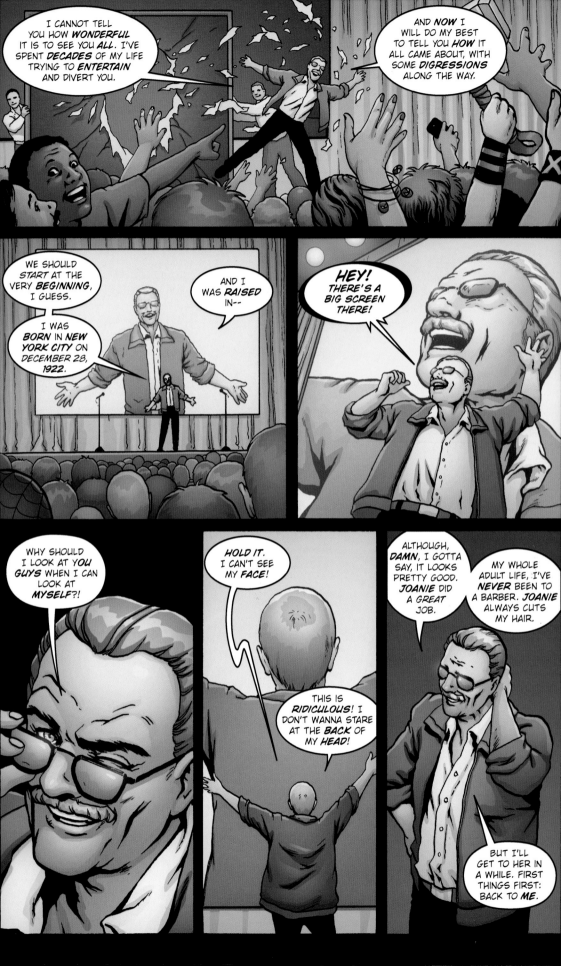

ANYWAY, I WAS **BORN** IN THE APARTMENT THAT I FIRST LIVED IN. MY FATHER WAS **JACK LIEBER**, MY MOTHER, **CELIA**. HE WAS A **ROMANIAN** IMMIGRANT WHO CAME TO THE **STATES** WHEN HE WAS YOUNG; MY MOM WAS BORN IN **NEW YORK**.

NINE YEARS LATER MY KID BROTHER, **LARRY**, WAS BORN. WE NEVER REALLY GOT A CHANCE TO **KNOW** EACH OTHER BECAUSE BY THE TIME HE WAS 5, I WAS 14 AND PLAYING WITH **OLDER** KIDS.

WE WERE LIVING IN **WASHINGTON HEIGHTS** BY THAT POINT, HAVING MOVED OUT OF THE APARTMENT ON **WEST 98TH STREET** AND **WEST END AVENUE**.

I'D SPEND MOST OF MY TIME **READING**.

I LOVED TO READ.

AND NOT **JUST** THAT, BUT MY MOTHER **LOVED** TO **WATCH** ME READ.

OR CHEW GUM.

OR **BREATHE**.

A Princess of Mars

I **PROBABLY** GOT MY SELF-CONFIDENCE FROM THE FACT THAT MY MOTHER THOUGHT **EVERYTHING** I DID WAS **BRILLIANT**.

I WAS **NEVER** HAPPY WITH OUR PLACE.

OUR ONLY VIEW WAS THE **BRICK WALL** OF THE REAR OF THE BUILDING NEXT TO US.

MY **DREAM** WAS TO ONE DAY BE **RICH** ENOUGH TO HAVE AN APARTMENT THAT FACED THE STREET.

DAD WAS A **DRESS CUTTER** BY TRADE, BUT HE SPENT MOST OF HIS TIME GOING THROUGH THE **WANT ADS**, LOOKING FOR WORK.

BUT IT WAS THE TIME OF THE **GREAT DEPRESSION**. THERE WAS **NO** WORK TO BE FOUND.

ANYTHING?

OF COURSE **NOT**. THERE'S **NEVER** ANYTHING.

I HAVE **ABSOLUTELY NO IDEA** HOW I'M GOING TO PAY THE **RENT** THIS MONTH.

I'D LIE THERE AT NIGHT, WISHING I WAS **OLDER** SO I COULD GET A JOB. BUT WHAT KIND OF JOB COULD I GET?

I FIGURED THAT IF I THOUGHT ABOUT IT HARD ENOUGH, I'D COME UP WITH SOMETHING.

SLAM

WATCH YOUR BROTHER.

IT WAS NOT THE BEST OF TIMES FOR US.

BUT DON'T GET ME *WRONG*, LIFE WASN'T *ALL* AWFUL.

TO THIS DAY, I THINK ABOUT MY FATHER SPENDING HIS TIME PAGING THROUGH THE NEWSPAPER'S WANT ADS IN FRUSTRATION...

...LOOKING FOR JOBS THAT WEREN'T THERE.

I MEAN, MY PARENTS *MUST* HAVE BEEN A FUN COUPLE AT SOME POINT.

BUT THEY SPENT A LOT OF TIME *ARGUING*, USUALLY ABOUT MONEY.

I'LL SAY THIS: IT GAVE ME A *HELL* OF A *WORK ETHIC*.

IT APPLIED TO SCHOOL AS WELL. I WORKED SO *HARD* I WOUND UP *SKIPPING GRADES*, WHICH MEANT I WAS TYPICALLY SURROUNDED BY *OLDER* KIDS.

EXCEPT DURING THE SUMMER, WHEN ALL THE KIDS WENT OFF TO CAMPS WITH COMPLICATED AMERICAN INDIAN NAMES.

THEN, THE STREETS WERE *DESERTED*. THAT WASN'T MUCH FUN.

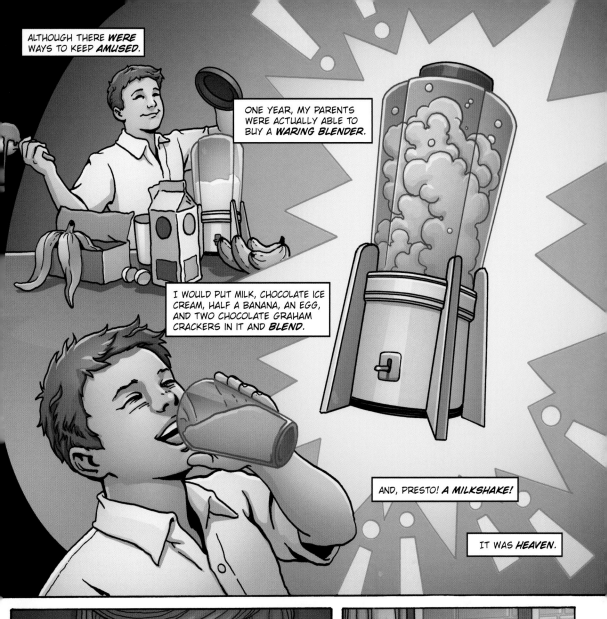

ALTHOUGH THERE *WERE* WAYS TO KEEP *AMUSED.*

ONE YEAR, MY PARENTS WERE ACTUALLY ABLE TO BUY A *WARING BLENDER.*

I WOULD PUT MILK, CHOCOLATE ICE CREAM, HALF A BANANA, AN EGG, AND TWO CHOCOLATE GRAHAM CRACKERS IN IT AND *BLEND.*

AND, PRESTO! *A MILKSHAKE!*

IT WAS *HEAVEN.*

OTHER THAN THAT, THOUGH...

There wasn't a lot to do.

I HAD A BALL. *THAT* WE COULD AFFORD.

SO I WOULD GO DOWN TO THE SCHOOL YARD HOPING TO FIND SOMEBODY TO PLAY *BALL* WITH.

BUT NO KIDS WERE AROUND ON THE WEEKENDS. BECAUSE MOST OF THEIR PARENTS HAD *CARS*...

SO THEY'D BE RIDING AROUND, *GOING PLACES*.

MY PARENTS COULDN'T AFFORD A CAR.

WE NEVER WENT *ANYWHERE*. MY LIFE WAS AT A DEAD END.

STAN... WE BOUGHT YOU SOMETHING.

YEAH?

THAT IS, UNTIL MY *TWELFTH* BIRTHDAY.

I'LL NEVER KNOW HOW THEY COULD *AFFORD* IT, BUT THAT *BIKE* BECAME MY BEST FRIEND.

I WOULD SPEND AS MUCH TIME AS I COULD AT THE **MOVIE THEATER**. I ESPECIALLY LOVED **ADVENTURE HEROES**...

...LIKE **ERROL FLYNN**, FOR INSTANCE. **THE ADVENTURES OF ROBIN HOOD** WAS ONE OF MY **FAVORITE** FILMS.

I WOULD IMAGINE **MYSELF** AS THE **HERO**, AND WHEN I'D COME OUT...

...I'D SEARCH FOR SOME **GIRL** WHO WAS BEING HARASSED SO THAT I COULD **RESCUE** HER!

WHICH **FORTUNATELY** I NEVER MANAGED, BECAUSE I'D PROBABLY HAVE GOTTEN MYSELF **KILLED**.

AS I GOT OLDER, I STARTED PICKING UP ODD JOBS IN ORDER TO MAKE **MONEY** AND HELP THE FAMILY.

I DELIVERED **LUNCHES** TO OFFICE WORKERS.

I WORKED IN A **NEWS OFFICE**, WRITING **OBITUARIES** IN ADVANCE FOR FAMOUS PEOPLE WHO WERE **STILL ALIVE!**

I QUIT THAT BECAUSE IT WAS TOO **DEPRESSING.**

I WROTE PUBLICITY FOR A **DENVER HOSPITAL.**

I NEVER KNEW IF I SHOULD BE ENCOURAGING PEOPLE TO GET **SICK** SO THEY'D GO TO THAT HOSPITAL.

I WORKED FOR A TROUSER MANUFACTURER.

NO ONE BOTHERED TO LEARN MY NAME. IF THEY WANTED ME, THEY'D JUST SHOUT...

BOY!

HATED THAT.

LUCKILY I GOT **FIRED** AFTER A FEW WEEKS.

MY **FAVORITE** EARLY JOB WAS AS AN USHER AT THE **RIVOLI THEATRE,** IN **TIMES SQUARE.** IT WAS MY **FIRST** JOB IN THE MOVIES.

AND I EVEN GOT TO **MEET** A **FAMOUS** PERSON.

ELEANOR ROOSEVELT, THE FIRST LADY, WAS VISITING OUR THEATER.

I WAS SO *PROUD* I THOUGHT MY HEAD WAS GOING TO *EXPLODE.*

SHE WALKED IN SURROUNDED BY FOUR SECRET SERVICE GUARDS.

THE THEATER HAD FOUR AVAILABLE AISLES AND SHE CHOSE *MINE!*

I WALKED DOWN THE AISLE, STIFF AS A *RAMROD...*

...AND *TRIPPED* OVER THE FOOT OF SOME *MORON* WHO HAD HIS LEG *STRETCHED* OUT IN THE AISLE.

BAM! DOWN I WENT.

ARE YOU *ALL RIGHT,* YOUNG MAN?

NOT MY PROUDEST MOMENT.

BUT THAT WAS *BEFORE* I WAS "*STAN LEE.*" LATER ENCOUNTERS WENT BETTER. I'LL GET TO THOSE IN A WHILE.

STAN! I WAS TALKING TO YOUR **UNCLE ROB** TODAY.

THE **PUBLISHING COMPANY** WHERE HE WORKS IS LOOKING FOR AN ASSISTANT.

YEAH?

WHAT DO THEY PUBLISH?

ALL DIFFERENT KINDS OF MAGAZINES.

"THEY'RE IN THE **McGRAW-HILL** BUILDING OVER ON **WEST 42ND STREET**."

WOW! YOU PUBLISH COMICS, TOO?

RIGHT! THAT, SON, IS **CAPTAIN AMERICA**...

...WRITTEN AND **CREATED** BY YOURS TRULY.

JOE SIMON. TIMELY COMICS' EDITOR. YOU'RE **STANLEY LIEBER**?

YES, SIR.

YOU KNOW WHAT A **COMICBOOK** IS?

ARE THEY LIKE COMIC STRIPS?

WELL, THE *FIRST* ONE WAS JUST THAT. IT WAS CALLED *FAMOUS FUNNIES*. CAME OUT ABOUT SEVEN YEARS AGO AND WAS A COLLECTION OF COMIC STRIPS.

SINCE THEN IT'S DEVELOPED INTO A *MAJOR* INDUSTRY, PUBLISHING ORIGINAL MATERIAL, INCLUDING *SUPER-HEROES* LIKE *CAP*.

I HEARD ABOUT *ONE* SUPERHERO. "*SUPERMAN*."

NO, THAT'S *NATIONAL PERIODICALS. SUPERMAN, BATMAN...*

Those are our *competition*.

BY THE WAY, HERE'S MY *ARTIST* AND CO-WRITER ON *CAPTAIN AMERICA...*

...*JACK KIRBY*.

IT WAS HARD TO *SEE* HIM THROUGH ALL THE *CIGAR* SMOKE.

AND *THAT'S* HOW IT *BEGAN!*

ACTUALLY, IT WAS A LOT OF *FUN*, BECAUSE EVERYTHING WAS *COOL* AND INFORMAL.

WHAT THE **HELL** IS THAT?

"YANKEE DOODLE DANDY." WANNA HEAR MORE? I'VE GOT *LOTS* OF 'EM.

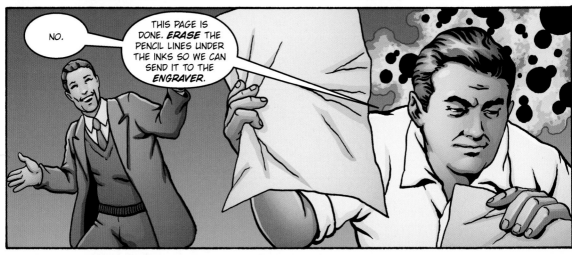

NO.

THIS PAGE IS DONE. *ERASE* THE PENCIL LINES UNDER THE INKS SO WE CAN SEND IT TO THE *ENGRAVER.*

THAT COULD BE A NEW HERO-- *"THE HUMAN ERASER"!*

WOW! MAYBE I SHOULD GET A *RAISE!*

WHAT? YOU'VE BEEN HERE A *WEEK!*

YEAH, BUT I DREAMED UP A *NEW* GUY FOR YOU!

STOP DREAMIN' AND PICK UP A TYPEWRITER. WE NEED A TWO-PAGE *CAPTAIN AMERICA* STORY-- TEXT ONLY.

Write it.

REALLY?!

YEAH. GET TO IT.

CAPTAIN AMERICA FOILS the TRAITOR'S REVENGE

By Stan Lee

WOW! I WAS FINALLY A *PROFESSIONAL* WRITER!

"*CAPTAIN AMERICA FOILS THE TRAITOR'S REVENGE.*" I EVEN MADE UP THE TITLE!

AND, YUP. USED A *PEN NAME.*

I JOINED THE ARMY. BECAUSE WRITING *PRETEND* STORIES ABOUT *CAP* GETTING THE JOB DONE *WASN'T* ENOUGH.

I *COULDN'T* WRITE *MAKE-BELIEVE* STORIES WHILE A REAL WAR WAS GOING ON.

BUT I NEVER HAD A CHANCE TO BE A HERO.

I WAS PUT IN THE SIGNAL CORPS AND STATIONED AT *FORT MONMOUTH, NEW JERSEY*, WHERE I STOOD GUARD OVER THE *ATLANTIC OCEAN* IN CASE THE *NAZIS* SHOWED UP.

I WAS COLD AND LONELY, AND THE ENEMY *NEVER* SHOWED UP.

NEXT THING I KNEW, I WAS TRANSFERRED TO A SPECIAL UNIT IN *ASTORIA, NEW YORK*.

IT SEEMS THEY LEARNED THAT I HAD BEEN A WRITER, SO THEY ASSIGNED ME TO THEIR TRAINING FILM DIVISION.

NOT QUITE THE *MACHO* IMAGE I HAD LONGED FOR, BUT I LEARNED TO *LIVE* WITH IT.

THERE I WAS, SHOULDER TO SHOULDER WITH WRITERS LIKE *WILLIAM SAROYAN*...

...*CHARLES ADDAMS*...

...*FRANK CAPRA*...

...*THEODOR GEISEL*, BETTER KNOWN AS *"DR. SEUSS"*...

...AND THE GUYS WHO WENT ON TO CREATE **CHARLIE'S ANGELS.**

SO **WHAT** WAS I WRITING? YOU ASK.

MOVIES FOR THE TROOPS! FILMS WITH **MEMORABLE** TITLES SUCH AS...

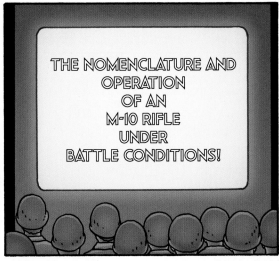

THE NOMENCLATURE AND OPERATION OF AN M-10 RIFLE UNDER BATTLE CONDITIONS!

THE G.I. METHOD OF ORGANIZING A FOOTLOCKER!

LIEBER! GOT NEWS FOR YOU.

NOTHING LEFT FOR YOU TO WRITE, SO YOU'RE BEING **TRANSFERRED.**

WHERE TO, **SARGE?**

WAGNER!

HERE!

ZAMBROSKI!

HERE!

ARE YOU SURE THERE'S *NOTHING* FOR ME? I'M EXPECTING A LETTER FROM *TIMELY COMICS*.

NAH. NOTHING.

THE NEXT DAY WAS SATURDAY. THE MAIL ROOM WAS CLOSED AND LOCKED. AND AS I WAS WALKING PAST...

MY LETTER *IS* THERE!

L

S. Lieber Benjamin Harrison
Fort Lawrence, Indiana

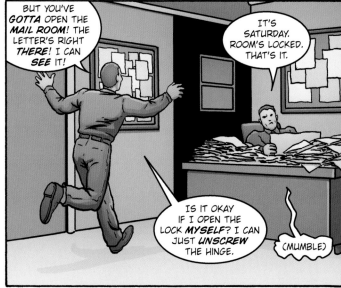

BUT YOU'VE *GOTTA* OPEN THE *MAIL ROOM!* THE LETTER'S RIGHT *THERE!* I CAN *SEE* IT!

IT'S SATURDAY. ROOM'S LOCKED. THAT'S IT.

IS IT OKAY IF I OPEN THE LOCK *MYSELF?* I CAN JUST *UNSCREW* THE HINGE.

(MUMBLE)

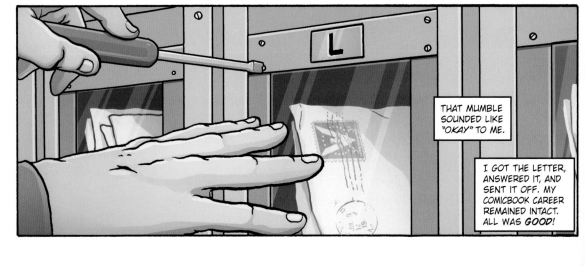

L

THAT MUMBLE SOUNDED LIKE "OKAY" TO ME.

I GOT THE LETTER, ANSWERED IT, AND SENT IT OFF. MY COMICBOOK CAREER REMAINED INTACT. ALL WAS *GOOD!*

LIEBER! REPORT TO THE COMPANY COMMANDER'S OFFICE, ON THE *DOUBLE!*

That doesn't sound good.

IT *WASN'T.*

YOU BROKE INTO THE *MAIL ROOM!*

ONLY TO TAKE *MY OWN* MAIL, SIR.

MAIL ROBBERY IS A *FEDERAL OFFENSE,* EVEN FOR *WISE-GUY* NEW YORKERS!

AS YOU WILL FIND OUT DURING YOUR STAY IN...

"LEAVENWORTH!"

CAPTAIN.

YES, *COLONEL!*

I AM *NOT* ABOUT TO LOSE MY ONE SIGNAL CORP WRITER. *FORGET* THIS *MINOR* MATTER AND CONCENTRATE ON WINNING THE WAR.

SIR! YES, SIR!

WHEEEWWWWW...

WHILE I WAS AWAY, *MARTIN* RELOCATED OUR OFFICES TO A LARGER SPACE IN THE *EMPIRE STATE BUILDING*. THAT WAS A RELIEF.

MY ARTIST FRIEND *VINCE FAGO* HAD BEEN *FILLING IN* FOR ME.

HEY, ANYONE NAMED *VINCE FAGO* 'ROUND HERE?

HUH?

STAN! YOU'RE BACK!

YEAH, I FINALLY *WON* THE WAR!

WOW! AM I *GLAD* TO SEE YOU! BEING EDITOR WAS *TOUGHER* THAN I THOUGHT!

AT *LAST* I CAN GO BACK TO BEING A CARTOONIST!

AND YOU WERE ALWAYS ONE OF THE *BEST*.

NOW THAT YOU'RE *BACK*, THINGS'LL START *HUMMING!*

I GOT MYSELF A PLACE AT THE *ALAMAC HOTEL* AND WENT BACK TO WRITING AND EDITING COMICBOOKS.

THERE IT WAS, *1947*, AND I WAS A FEW DAYS SHY OF MY *TWENTY-FIFTH* BIRTHDAY.

AND WHAT A *BIRTHDAY* PRESENT I GOT! A FRIEND SET ME UP FOR A BLIND DATE WITH A *MODEL!*

I HAD NO IDEA WHAT TO EXPECT. THAT'S KIND OF THE *POINT* OF BLIND DATES, I GUESS.

"COMPANY WHOSE NAME I DON'T REMEMBER"

AFTER THREE YEARS AT ARMY CAMPS, I COULDN'T *WAIT* TO SEE HER!

SHE WASN'T *JUST* A "HER."

SHE WAS A *VISION!*

MAY I *HELP* YOU?

SHE *WASN'T* EVEN THE MODEL I WAS *SUPPOSED* TO MEET!

BUT I KNEW--*SHE* WAS THE ONE I *WANTED!*

SEE, HERE'S THE THING ABOUT *MEMORY*. IT'S *NOT* LINEAR.

YOU'RE TALKING ABOUT ONE THING AND IT REMINDS YOU OF *ANOTHER* THING AND THEN YOU HAVE TO GO *BACK*.

TO APPRECIATE MY REACTION TO SEEING *JOAN*, YOU HAVE TO UNDERSTAND THAT I'D BEEN *DRAWING* HER.

FOR *YEARS*.

SHE WAS MY *DREAM* GIRL, YOU SEE. I DID COUNTLESS DRAWINGS OF HER OVER THE YEARS--AND I'M NOT EVEN AN *ARTIST*!

AHHHHH!

WHO ARE YOU?!?

YOUR WORK--HOW DO YOU *DO* IT?

I MEAN, I'D FIGURE THE *ARTIST* WRITES THE COMIC. WHAT DO THEY NEED *YOU* FOR?

WELL, *HERE.* MAYBE THIS'LL HELP.

HERE'S *YOU.* YOU'RE THE ONE WHO COMES UP WITH THE *BASIC IDEA.*

LIKE, YOU'D SAY, "OKAY, IN *THIS* ISSUE *DOCTOR DOOM* TAKES OVER THE *BAXTER BUILDING!* AND ONLY *DAREDEVIL* IS THE *FF'S* ALLY!"

WHO ARE--?

JUST *GO* WITH IT.

YOU SIT DOWN WITH THE ARTIST, *JACK KIRBY.* YOU TELL THIS PREMISE TO HIM.

HE GOES OFF AND *DESIGNS* THE STORY.

BECAUSE I'M *WRITING* WAY *TOO MANY* BOOKS A MONTH.

BESIDES, I'M A *LOUSY* ARTIST!

WHY DON'T *YOU* DO THAT?

YOU GET THE ARTWORK BACK FROM *JACK* AND YOU SIT DOWN AND *TYPE* THE SCRIPT.

SCRIPT?

WORD BALLOONS. *SOUND EFFECTS. EVERY* WORD ON THE PAGE COMES FROM *YOU.*

YOU ALSO DRAW IN THE WORD BALLOONS AND SOUND EFFECTS AND NUMBER THEM ON THE PAGE, AND THAT GOES TO THE *LETTERER.*

HE LETTERS IN YOUR SCRIPT.

Letterer

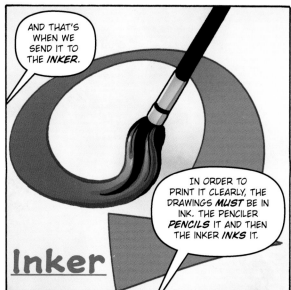

AND THAT'S WHEN WE SEND IT TO THE *INKER.*

IN ORDER TO PRINT IT CLEARLY, THE DRAWINGS *MUST* BE IN INK. THE PENCILER *PENCILS* IT AND THEN THE INKER *INKS* IT.

Inker

AND THEN THE *COLORIST* COLORS PHOTOCOPIES OF IT--

PHOTO *WHAT?*

COPIES OF THE ARTWORK. AND THOSE ARE THEN SENT TO THE *PRINTER.*

AND THEN IT GETS A COVER AND IS *PUBLISHED* INTO A COMICBOOK.

Colorist

OH, *WAIT!* YOU MEAN LIKE *THIS?*

KIND OF. BUT I LIKE *OURS* BETTER.

You don't need to save that. It probably won't be worth anything.

ANYWAY, YOU **DON'T** BECOME **PRESIDENT**. BUT YOU **MEET** A BUNCH OF THEM. AND YOU ALSO MEET **HER**.

OH **YEAH**! WANNA **HEAR** ABOUT HER?

I **DO**? SHE'S **REAL**?

SURE.

HER NAME IS **JOAN BOOCOCK**.

BRITISH, FROM A PLACE CALLED **NEWCASTLE UPON TYNE**.

I...WE... FALL IN **LOVE** WITH HER THE **MOMENT** WE SEE HER.

We play it **COOL**, of course.

I THINK I'M IN **LOVE** WITH YOU.

WELL, ISN'T THAT **SWEET**.

YOU WANT TO **GO OUT**? RIGHT **NOW**?

WAIT...ARE YOU THE FELLOW WHO'S SUPPOSED TO BE DATING **BETTY**?

WHO?

I NEVER ACTUALLY MET **BETTY**. IN A SHORT TIME, **JOANIE** AND I WERE GOING STEADY.

ONE OF OUR **FAVORITE** PLACES TO GO WAS THE BEACH. WE **LOVED** THE BEACH.

FINALLY, AFTER A COUPLE DATES...

...WE JUST **KNEW** WE WERE GONNA GET **MARRIED**.

HERE WAS THE *PROBLEM*: TECHNICALLY, *JOANIE* WAS STILL *MARRIED* TO SOMEONE ELSE. SHE HAD ALREADY WANTED TO GET A *DIVORCE*.

AND IT SEEMED TO HER THAT THE *BEST* PLACE TO GO GET ONE WAS...

RENO.

YOU ONLY HAD TO WAIT *SIX WEEKS* FOR A DIVORCE TO BE PROCESSED.

HERE WAS THE NEXT PROBLEM: WHILE I WAS ON MY *OWN* IN *NEW YORK CITY*...

...*JOAN* WAS THE SUBJECT OF, SHALL WE SAY, A GOOD DEAL OF *ATTENTION* IN *RENO*.

MATTERS CAME TO A HEAD A FEW WEEKS LATER WHEN SHE WROTE ME A VERY LOVING, CONVERSATIONAL LETTER.

THE *ISSUE* WAS HOW SHE STARTED IT.

DEAR *JACK?!?*

YOU READING LEFTOVER MAIL TO *KIRBY?*

NO, IT'S FROM *JOANIE!* SHE *ACCIDENTALLY* CALLED ME *"JACK."*

AT LEAST I *HOPE* IT WAS ACCIDENTAL!

MIGHT WANT TO DO SOMETHING ABOUT THAT...

...BEFORE SHE COMES BACK FROM *RENO* WITH ANOTHER GUY ON HER ARM AND A *RING* ON HER FINGER.

OKAY, THAT LAST CONVERSATION MAY NOT HAVE HAPPENED, BUT YOU GET THE DRIFT.

ANYWAY, OFF I WENT TO MY LOCAL AIRPORT.

I WANT A TICKET ON THE *FIRST* PLANE LEAVING FOR *RENO!*

THAT WAS A MISTAKE, BECAUSE THE *IDIOT* TICKET SELLER TOOK ME *LITERALLY.*

TICKETS

HERE'S YOUR TICKET, SIR!

TICKET

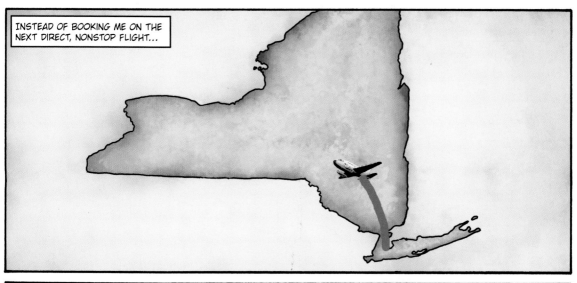

INSTEAD OF BOOKING ME ON THE NEXT DIRECT, NONSTOP FLIGHT...

...HE PUT ME ON A DC-3 THAT MADE *THREE* STOPS BEFORE IT EVEN GOT OUT OF NEW YORK.

IT THEN WENT ON TO STOP AT EVERY FLYSPECK TOWN BEFORE FINALLY MAKING IT TO *NEVADA*.

TWENTY-EIGHT HOURS IT TOOK TO GET TO *RENO*.

SO I COME STAGGERING OFF THE PLANE.

Holy...

WELCOME TO RENO.

JOANIE LATER TOLD ME THAT WHEN SHE SAW ME *STUMBLING* OFF THE PLANE, LOOKING LIKE A *LOST BOY SCOUT* AMONG ALL THOSE *RUGGED* COWBOY TYPES, SHE WONDERED WHAT SHE WAS GETTING HERSELF *INTO*.

WISELY ENOUGH...

...I DIDN'T GIVE HER *ANY* TIME TO THINK ABOUT IT.

SINCE THE SIX WEEKS WERE UP, WE WENT STRAIGHT TO THE OFFICE OF THE JUDGE WHO GRANTED *DIVORCES*.

BUT I'D SEEN THE LAY OF THE LAND, SO I WAS NOT GONNA *WASTE* ANY TIME.

WE WENT RIGHT NEXT DOOR. IT WAS THE *SAME* JUDGE; HE JUST HAD TWO DIFFERENT ROOMS FOR DIVORCES AND MARRIAGES.

THERE WAS ANOTHER YOUNG COUPLE THERE, ALSO WAITING TO GET MARRIED. SO WE AGREED TO BE EACH OTHER'S WITNESSES.

EACH CEREMONY TOOK *SIXTY SECONDS* AT MOST.

WE WERE ALL SO *EMOTIONAL* THAT WE SWORE WE WOULD MEET UP EVERY YEAR ON OUR *ANNIVERSARY* TO SEE HOW WE WERE DOING.

AND DO YOU KNOW WHO THOSE TWO PEOPLE *WERE*?!

SERIOUSLY. I'M ASKING.

Because I got *no* clue.

WITHIN *FIVE MINUTES* THEIR NAMES HAD GONE OUT OF OUR HEADS AND WE *NEVER* SAW THEM AGAIN.

How temporal is transient sentiment.

WE TOOK THE TRAIN BACK TO *NEW YORK*, BECAUSE I'D PRETTY MUCH *HAD IT* WITH AIRPLANES FOR A WHILE.

AND THEN THERE WERE SOME VERY *IMPORTANT* PEOPLE FOR ME TO INTRODUCE MY EPISCOPALIAN MODEL WIFE TO.

MOM, DAD, THIS IS *JOANIE*... MY *WIFE.*

WELCOME TO THE FAMILY. I *ALWAYS* WANTED A DAUGHTER.

GOOD JOB, *SON.* SHE'S *GORGEOUS.*

• *WHEEWWWWW* •

SO THERE WE WERE IN 1947. EVERYTHING WAS *GREAT.*

WELL...NOT *EVERYTHING.*

SO, **STAN**...WHAT DO YOU DO FOR A LIVING?

I'M A WRITER. EXCUSE ME.

WHAT KIND OF A WRITER?

CHILDREN'S LITERATURE.

REALLY! WHAT **KIND** OF CHILDREN'S LITERATURE?

ANYTHING I MIGHT HAVE READ TO MY KIDS OR--?

COMICBOOKS.

IN THOSE DAYS, THAT WAS THE KIND OF RESPONSE COMICS GOT. IF NOT OUTRIGHT HOSTILITY.

FREDRIC WERTHAM.

HE WAS A GERMAN-BORN PSYCHOLOGIST WHO RAN A LOW-COST CLINIC THAT MOSTLY CATERED TO YOUNG UNDERPRIVILEGED CHILDREN.

DURING THAT TIME, HE MET A LOT OF *JUVENILE DELINQUENTS*, *MOST* OF WHOM READ COMICS. OF COURSE, SO DID MILLIONS OF *NON-JDS*, BUT *DR. WERTHAM* DIDN'T CARE ABOUT THEM.

INSTEAD, HE CONCLUDED THAT COMICS *CAUSED* CHILDREN TO FALL INTO LIVES OF *CRIME*.

IN FACT, HE WROTE A BOOK ABOUT IT:

the author of THE SHOW OF VIOLENCE and DARK LEGEND

SEDUCTION
OF THE
INNOCENT

Fredric Wertham, M. D.

AND *THAT* BOOK, IN TURN, IN THE YEAR *1954*, LED HIM TO TESTIFY IN FRONT OF A *SENATE SUBCOMMITTEE* ON JUVENILE DELINQUENCY...

...LED BY ONE *ESTES KEFAUVER*, A TENNESSEE DEMOCRAT WHO, SOME SAID, WAS USING THE PUBLICITY TO ANGLE FOR A RUN AT THE *PRESIDENCY*.

WERTHAM ALSO HAD GUYS WORKING UNDER HIM, SPREADING THE WORD ON THE *DANGERS* OF COMICS.

I ATTENDED ONE OF THEIR MEETINGS JUST OUT OF *CURIOSITY*.

EXPOSURE TO *THESE SORTS* OF TALES IS SENDING YOUR CHILDREN RIGHT DOWN THE *SEWERS!*

LET ME SHOW YOU *ANOTHER* ONE.

THIS WAS PUBLISHED BY *TIMELY/ATLAS COMICS.* HAVE ANY OF YOU *HEARD* OF THEM?

THEY PUBLISH VARIOUS SUPERHERO TITLES GOING BACK TO THE 1930S. BUT *DR. WERTHAM* CONSIDERS THIS ONE *ESPECIALLY APPALLING.*

NOTICE, IF YOU WILL, THE *SEXUAL SUGGESTION.* THE LONG, *HARD* NECK EXTENDED *THROUGH* THE *HOLE.* CHILDREN CLEARLY *KNOW* WHAT IS GOING ON HERE.

What is he talking about?

I HAVE *NO* IDEA.

whewww

BUT THAT WASN'T ENOUGH TO DETER THE PUBLISHERS FROM CAVING IN, ESPECIALLY AFTER *BILL GAINES*, PUBLISHER OF HORROR COMICS, DELIVERED SOME PRETTY *UNPOPULAR* TESTIMONY.

A COVER IN BAD TASTE, FOR EXAMPLE, MIGHT BE DEFINED AS HOLDING THE HEAD A LITTLE HIGHER SO THAT THE NECK COULD BE SEEN DRIPPING BLOOD FROM IT, AND MOVING THE BODY OVER A LITTLE FARTHER SO THAT THE NECK OF THE BODY COULD BE SEEN TO BE BLOODY.

PARTLY TO DRIVE *GAINES* OUT OF BUSINESS AND PARTLY TO COVER THEIR *OWN* BUTTS, THE PUBLISHERS CREATED THE *COMICS CODE AUTHORITY* IN 1954.

APPROVED BY THE COMICS CODE AUTHORITY

A SEAL WENT ON EVERY COVER...

...TO GUARANTEE THAT *ALL* COMICS PUBLISHED STUCK TO A *STRICT* RULE OF GUIDELINES THAT PRODUCED *"SAFE"* COMICS.

THIS PRETTY MUCH *KILLED* DISTRIBUTION FOR ALL OF *GAINES'S* HORROR AND CRIME COMICS.

FORTUNATELY, HE FOUND A WAY TO BOUNCE BACK.

AS FOR *ME*, WELL, AS WE ROLLED INTO THE *1960S*, WE CHANGED OUR NAME TO *MARVEL COMICS*, LEAVING BEHIND THE *ATLAS* DAYS.

I KNEW THAT YOUNG PEOPLE WERE READING THESE BOOKS, AND HAD THERE NOT BEEN A *CODE*, I DON'T THINK THAT I WOULD HAVE DONE THE COMICS ANY DIFFERENTLY.

I WAS INTERESTED IN CREATING STORIES THAT HAD *HUMAN* CHARACTERS THAT COULD BE *RELATABLE* NO MATTER *WHAT* THE READER'S AGE.

HOWEVER, IN *1971* I GOT A LETTER FROM THE DEPARTMENT OF HEALTH, EDUCATION, AND WELFARE THAT ACCIDENTALLY LED ME TO HAVE TO *CHALLENGE* THE *CODE*.

GIL KANE.

WHAT'S IT SAY, **STAN**?

IT SAYS THAT THEY'RE CONCERNED ABOUT **DRUG** USE AMONG KIDS. AND SINCE **MARVEL** HAS SO MUCH INFLUENCE ON YOUNG PEOPLE, THEY THINK WE SHOULD PUT AN **ANTI-DRUG** MESSAGE IN OUR BOOKS.

SO YOU WANT TO...**WHAT**? PUBLISH A **SPECIAL ISSUE** OR SOMETHING?

NO, NO. I DON'T WANT TO MAKE IT LIKE A **SERMON**. LIKE WE'RE **PREACHING** TO THEM BECAUSE IT'S A **CAPTIVE** AUDIENCE.

WE'VE GOT TO **INJECT** THE THEME OF **DRUG ADDICTION** AS A PERIPHERAL SUBPLOT THAT WON'T **DILUTE** THE **ACTION** OR **DRAMA** OR **SUSPENSE** OF THE REGULAR **SUPERHERO** THEME.

GOT IT! WE'LL DO A THREE-PART **SPIDER-MAN** STORY.

WE CAN HAVE **NORMAN OSBORN** REGAIN HIS MEMORY. THAT'S THE **MAIN** PLOT.

BUT THAT'S GOT **NOTHING** TO DO WITH **DRUGS**.

YEAH, I KNOW! BUT WE'LL HAVE THIS **SUBPLOT** THAT'S GOT **HARRY** POPPING PILLS BECAUSE HE'S **UPSET** THAT **MJ DUMPED HIM!**

OH, AND EARLY ON, WE'LL HAVE THIS GUY **STONED** OUT OF HIS MIND AND HE JUMPS OFF A ROOF, BUT **SPIDEY SAVES** HIM.

AND WE CAN HAVE **PETER** SAY...

MY LIFE AS **SPIDER-MAN** IS PROBABLY AS **DANGEROUS** AS ANY...

...BUT I'D RATHER FACE A **HUNDRED SUPERVILLAINS** THAN TOSS IT **AWAY** BY GETTING HOOKED ON HARD DRUGS! 'CAUSE THAT'S **ONE** FIGHT YOU **CAN'T** WIN!

THAT SOUNDS GREAT, *STAN!*

GLAD YOU LIKE IT, *GIL!* 'CAUSE *YOU'RE* GONNA *DRAW* IT!

I AM? BUT I'M NOT THE REGULAR ARTIST.

YOU ARE *NOW.* DIDN'T I MENTION? WE NEED A NEW PENCILER.

AND *GIL KANE* DID DRAW IT *EXACTLY* AS WE IMAGINED IT. BUT THEN WE RAN INTO A *SNAG* WHEN THE BOOK WAS SUBMITTED TO THE CCA.

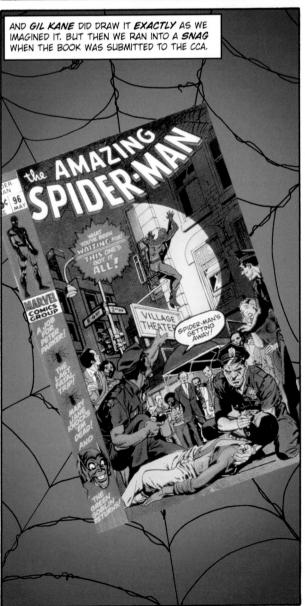

YOU CAN'T DO THIS STORY.

WHY?

ACCORDING TO THE RULES OF THE CODE, YOU *CAN'T* MENTION DRUGS IN A STORY.

LOOK, WE'RE NOT TELLING KIDS TO *TAKE* DRUGS! THIS IS AN *ANTI*-DRUG THEME!

IT DOESN'T *MATTER.* YOU MENTION DRUGS.

BUT A GOVERNMENT AGENCY *ASKED* US TO DO IT!

APPROVED BY THE COMICS CODE AUTHORITY

IT DOESN'T MATTER. YOU CAN'T MENTION DRUGS.

BUT THE WORD "DRUGS" ISN'T CONTAINED *ANYWHERE* IN YOUR BOOK OF RULES. THERE'S *NOTHING* HERE THAT SPECIFICALLY SAYS WE *CAN'T* MENTION *DRUGS!*

APPROVED BY THE COMICS CODE CA AUTHORITY

YOU'RE FORGETTING *STANDARDS, PART C*, AND I QUOTE...

..."ALL ELEMENTS OR TECHNIQUES NOT SPECIFICALLY MENTIONED HEREIN, BUT WHICH ARE CONTRARY TO THE SPIRIT AND INTENT OF THE CODE, AND ARE CONSIDERED VIOLATIONS OF GOOD TASTE OR DECENCY, SHALL BE PROHIBITED."

HOW IS AN *ANTI*-DRUG STORY A *VIOLATION* OF GOOD TASTE OR DECENCY?!

BECAUSE IT MENTIONS DRUGS!

THIS COMIC IS IN VIOLATION OF THE CCA AND WILL *NOT* CARRY THE SEAL!

WHAAAAM!

MARTIN, YOU *HAVE* TO LET ME SEND THESE THREE ISSUES *WITHOUT* THE *CODE SEAL* OF APPROVAL.

GOSH, *STAN*, THAT'S TAKING A *BIG STEP*. I MEAN, WE'RE SUPPOSED TO *ABIDE* BY THE *CODE*.

YEAH, BUT A BRANCH OF THE *US GOVERNMENT* WANTS THIS STORY--AND THAT *TOPS* THE CCA!

AND *BESIDES*, THIS IS A *GOOD THING*. IT'S LETTING KIDS KNOW THAT DRUGS ARE *HARMFUL*.

OKAY, *STAN*. YOU *GO AHEAD* AND DO IT AND I'LL BACK YOU UP.

A Comics Magazine Defies Code Ban on Drug Stories

By LAWRENCE VAN GELDER

For the first time since its adoption 16 years ago, the Code of the Comics Magazine Association of America, which governs the contents of more than 300 million comic books published each year in the United States, has been overhauled.

As a result of revisions adopted last week, comic books now deal more easily with criminal acts by government officials and the police, with sex, with contemporary language and with the occult.

However, despite considerable pressure from some publishers and editors within the industry, the code continues to make no specific provision for dealing with drug abuse.

Published Without Seal

Although a traditional ban on such stories remains, one publisher has defied the prohibition to publish without the code's seal of approval a comic book containing a story line dealing disapprovingly with drug abuse.

The May issue of The Amazing Spider-Man, published by the Marvel Comics Group of Magazine Management Company, a subsidiary

APPROVED BY THE COMICS CODE AUTHORITY

Seal of the Comics Magazine Association, which governs content of most comic books published in the United States.

of Cadence Industries at 625 Madison Avenue, marks the first time since adoption of the code that a subscribing member has published without its seal of approval.

The code was adopted by publishers of 90 per cent of the nation's comic books on Oct. 26, 1954, a period when comic books came under attack by psychologists, legislators and educators. The resulting code governed Hollywood for many years. The strict Code sharply

tion of violence, gore and sex in comic books.

Consistent violation of the code could mean expulsion from membership in the Comics Magazine Association, accompanied by notification of newsdealers, many of whom presumably would decline to handle the publishers' wares. In essence, the code is regarded by all its subscribing members as a beneficial standard, safeguarding their industry and prompting their allegiance.

Stan Lee, the editor of Spider-Man, said he was impelled to proceed with a story containing a subplot on drug abuse by a letter he received from an official of the National Institute of Mental Health, a branch of the Department of Health, Education and Welfare.

Reason for Action

The letter suggested, in part, that a public service could be performed by assisting in the dissemination of factual information on drug abuse.

WHICH IT *DID*, I SUPPOSE. ALTHOUGH THE *TIMES* MADE IT SOUND LIKE WE WERE *PUSHING* DRUGS.

BUT IT WAS THE BEGINNING OF THE END FOR THE *CCA*. GRANTED, IT TOOK ANOTHER *FORTY YEARS*, BUT WHEN THE WORLD DIDN'T COME *CRASHING DOWN* WHILE OUR *CCA*-LESS TITLES CAME OUT...

BY THE COMICS CODE AUTHORITY

...WELL, EVENTUALLY *EVERYONE* STARTED IGNORING IT (*DC* DIDN'T GIVE UP THE *SEAL* UNTIL 2011) AND IT WENT *DEFUNCT*.

YOU KNOW *WHAT*? I'VE GOTTEN *WAY* AHEAD OF MYSELF.

I STARTED TALKING ABOUT THE *CCA* AND JUST GOT PULLED FORWARD AND BEGAN TALKING ABOUT *SPIDER-MAN* EVEN THOUGH I HADN'T EVEN GOTTEN TO WHERE I *DREAMED* HIM UP YET.

LET'S *BACKTRACK*.

JOAN AND I MOVED OUT TO *LONG ISLAND* AFTER LIVING IN *MANHATTAN* FOR A COUPLE OF YEARS AS NEWLYWEDS.

THINGS WERE GOING *GREAT*. BUT THEN, SADLY, MY MOTHER PASSED AWAY.

SO MY BROTHER, *LARRY*, MOVED IN WITH US.

BUT AFTER A WHILE, *LARRY* FELT IT WOULD BE BETTER IF HE *MOVED ON* AND, ONCE HE WAS OLD ENOUGH TO LIVE ON HIS OWN, HE *DID*.

IN APRIL OF 1950, *JOAN* GAVE BIRTH TO OUR FIRST DAUGHTER.

WE SHOULD CALL HER *JOAN.* AFTER *YOU.*

ACTUALLY...

...I WAS THINKING *CELIA,* AFTER YOUR *MOTHER.*

HOW ABOUT *JOAN CELIA?*

THAT SOUNDS *WONDERFUL.*

WOULD YOU LIKE TO HOLD HER?

JUST TRY TO *STOP* ME.

Hey, *J.C.* I'm your *daddy.*

AND THEN, IN *1953*, WE HAD A *SECOND* DAUGHTER. HER NAME WAS *JAN*. AND SHE...

...UHM...

SHE DIED. THREE DAYS OLD.

Never even left the hospital.

IT HIT *JOAN* TERRIBLY HARD, AS YOU CAN IMAGINE. LUCKILY, WE WERE BOTH THERE FOR EACH OTHER AND *SOMEHOW* GOT THROUGH IT.

LATER WE TRIED TO *ADOPT*, BUT THE WHOLE PROCESS WAS TOO *PAINFUL*.

TO MAKE THINGS EVEN *WORSE*--

THE DOCTOR SAID *JOANIE* COULDN'T HAVE ANOTHER CHILD.

LET'S NOT DWELL ON IT.

THE TYPES OF BOOKS WE WERE ABLE TO PRODUCE BACK THEN WERE *CRIPPLED* BY THE *CCA*, BUT WE STILL HAD *GREAT* ARTISTS.

DAN DeCARLO...

...AL JAFFEE...

...GENE COLAN...

...AND THEN THERE WAS *JOE MANEELY*.

WISHT I WASN'T ALWAYS THE *LITTLEST!*

HE WAS THE *CO-CREATOR* OF SEVERAL CHARACTERS I'M *SURE* YOU REMEMBER...

...SUCH AS THE *BLACK KNIGHT*...

...THE *RINGO KID*...

...AND THE *YELLOW CLAW* AND *JIMMY WOO*. THE CLAW WOULD GO ON TO BATTLE *CAPTAIN AMERICA* AND JIMMY WOO WOUND UP JOINING *S.H.I.E.L.D.*

MAN...*SO* MUCH STUFF HAS HAPPENED IN COMICS DURING MY TIME.

AND JUST THINK: I *ALMOST* WASN'T THERE FOR IT.

BECAUSE BY THE EARLY SIXTIES I'D ABOUT *HAD IT.* I WAS *TIRED* OF COMICS AND WAS WORKING ON MY OWN HUMOR BOOKS. I ALWAYS *LOVED* WRITING HUMOR.

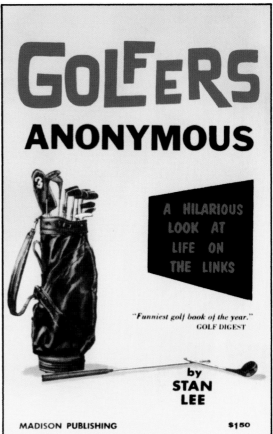

GOLFERS ANONYMOUS

A HILARIOUS LOOK AT LIFE ON THE LINKS

"*Funniest golf book of the year.*"
GOLF DIGEST

by STAN LEE

MADISON PUBLISHING $1.50

SNAFU WAS OUR ANSWER TO *MAD* MAGAZINE. I WROTE THE FIRST ISSUE MYSELF.

Snafu
HE WHO LAUGHS — LASTS!

MARCH
25¢
EASY TERMS AVAILABLE
ATLAS

Big Rugged-Action Issue

IN FACT, THERE WAS A FAMOUS MAGAZINE CALLED THE *SATURDAY EVENING POST* THAT HAD THE LINE "FOUNDED BY BENJAMIN FRANKLIN." SO ON THE CONTENTS PAGE OF *SNAFU* IT READ...

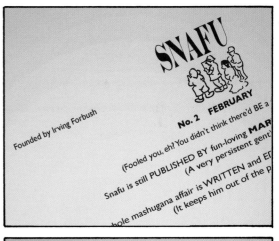

SNAFU
No. 2 FEBRUARY

Founded by Irving Forbush

(Fooled you, eh? You didn't think there'd BE a

Snafu is still PUBLISHED BY fun-loving MAR
(A very persistent gent)

hole mashugana affair is WRITTEN and EF

(It keeps him out of the p

...AND ON THE *OTHER* SIDE...

SNAFU
No. 2 FEBRUARY

Losted by Marvin Forbush

didn't think there'd BE a second issue

BY fun-loving MARTIN G
y persistent gent)

TTEN and EDITED by smiling STAN LEE
ut of the pool room)

HEY, WHATTAYA WANT? IT ONLY COST A *QUARTER.*

STILL...

MARTIN HAD STARTED HIS OWN DISTRIBUTION ARM, *THE ATLAS NEWS COMPANY*, AND WE'D MOVED OUT OF THE *EMPIRE STATE BUILDING*.

EVENTUALLY THINGS WENT SOUTH AND *ATLAS DISTRIBUTION* COLLAPSED. WE STILL CALLED THE COMICS *ATLAS* FOR A WHILE...BUT IT WASN'T LIKE THERE WERE A TON OF COMICS BEING PRODUCED.

NO, *JOHNNY*, I'M *SORRY*, WE'VE *NO WORK* RIGHT NOW.

WE'VE TRIMMED *WAY BACK* ON OUR COMICS.

I DUNNO. TRY *DC COMICS*.

DC.

THEY *USED* TO BE *NATIONAL*, BUT *NOW* THEY'RE *DC*.

I HEAR THEIR *JUSTICE LEAGUE* BOOK IS DOING WELL.

SHEESH.

I'D READ *JUSTICE LEAGUE*. THE HEROES WEREN'T WRITTEN IN MY STYLE AND HAD NO PERSONAL PROBLEMS. BUT THE BOOK SEEMED TO BE *SUCCESSFUL*.

THAT WAS *ALL* MOST SUPERHEROES WERE, REALLY. *SUPERBEINGS* WITH VERY LITTLE CONNECTION TO *REAL* HUMANITY.

BETWEEN *THAT* AND OUR OWN OBSESSION WITH *JUVENILE* STORIES AND LANGUAGE...

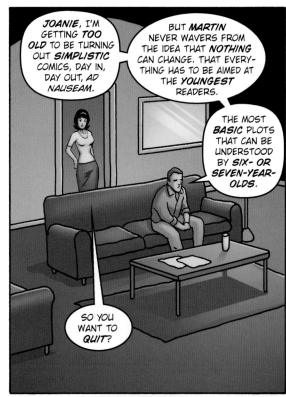

JOANIE, I'M GETTING *TOO OLD* TO BE TURNING OUT *SIMPLISTIC* COMICS, DAY IN, DAY OUT, *AD NAUSEAM*.

BUT *MARTIN* NEVER WAVERS FROM THE IDEA THAT *NOTHING* CAN CHANGE. THAT EVERY- THING HAS TO BE AIMED AT THE *YOUNGEST* READERS.

THE MOST *BASIC* PLOTS THAT CAN BE UNDERSTOOD BY *SIX- OR SEVEN-YEAR- OLDS*.

SO YOU WANT TO *QUIT*?

YEAH, PRETTY MUCH.

ALTHOUGH...

ALTHOUGH WHAT?

WELL... *MARTIN* WAS PLAYING GOLF TODAY WITH *JACK LIEBOWITZ*.

THE PUBLISHER OF *DC COMICS*?

YEAH.

SO THIS *JUSTICE LEAGUE* COMICBOOK WE'RE PUBLISHING...IT'S TAKING OFF LIKE A *ROCKET*!

LOOKS LIKE SUPERHEROES MIGHT BE COMING BACK *FINALLY*!

REAAAALLY?

STAN, CAN YOU COME UP WITH A TEAM OF *SUPERHEROES* LIKE THE *JUSTICE LEAGUE*?

WELL, I--

YOU COULD USE OUR OLD *HUMAN TORCH* AND *SUB-MARINER* AND MAYBE *CAPTAIN AMERICA*!

THAT'LL SAVE YOU FROM HAVING TO DREAM UP NEW CHARACTERS!

WHAT DO YOU *SAY*?

WHAT *DID* YOU SAY?

I SAID I'D THINK ABOUT IT. BUT REALLY, WHAT'S THE *POINT*? I *DON'T WANT* TO JUST KEEP RECYCLING *OLD* CHARACTERS.

I FEEL LIKE *QUITTING*.

LOOK, *STAN*, IF YOU WANT TO QUIT, YOU *KNOW* I'LL SUPPORT YOU.

BUT THINK ABOUT *THIS*:

IF *MARTIN* WANTS YOU TO CREATE A *NEW GROUP* OF SUPERHEROES, THIS COULD BE THE CHANCE FOR YOU TO DO IT THE WAY YOU'VE *ALWAYS WANTED TO*.

YOU COULD DREAM UP PLOTS THAT HAVE **MORE DEPTH** AND **SUBSTANCE** TO THEM, AND **CREATE CHARACTERS** THAT HAVE **INTERESTING PERSONALITIES**, WHO SPEAK LIKE **REAL** PEOPLE.

IT MIGHT BE FUN FOR YOU TO CREATE **BRAND-NEW** HEROES AND WRITE THEM IN A **DIFFERENT STYLE**, THE STYLE YOU'VE **ALWAYS** WANTED TO USE...

...ONE THAT MIGHT ATTRACT **OLDER** READERS AS WELL AS THE YOUNGER ONES.

REMEMBER, YOU'VE GOT **NOTHING TO LOSE** BY DOING THE BOOK **YOUR WAY**.

THE **WORST** THAT CAN HAPPEN IS THAT **MARTIN** GETS **MAD** AND **FIRES** YOU. BUT YOU WANT TO **QUIT** ANYWAY, SO **WHAT'S THE RISK**? AT LEAST YOU'LL'VE GOTTEN IT OUT OF YOUR SYSTEM.

YOU'RE **RIGHT**! WHAT'S THE **WORST** THAT CAN HAPPEN?

TO THE TYPEWRITER!

THE FIRST THING TO DO IS START WITH *MARTIN'S* SUGGESTION. KICK OFF THE TEAM WITH THE *HUMAN TORCH.*

THE *TORCH* FIRST SHOWED UP IN 1939 IN *MARVEL COMICS* #1. IN A STORY CREATED BY *CARL BURGOS*, WE FIRST MET THE ANDROID CRAFTED BY *PHINEAS HORTON* WHO COULD TURN INTO *FLAME.*

IN FACT...

...EAGLE-EYED FANS SPOTTED HIM IN A CAMEO APPEARANCE IN THE FIRST *CAPTAIN AMERICA* MOVIE DURING THE FAIR SEQUENCE.

SO HE WAS CERTAINLY A GOOD STARTING PLACE FOR MY HERO TEAM.

BUT I DIDN'T WANT TO JUST REPRODUCE THE ANDROID *TORCH.*

I DECIDED TO *UPDATE* HIM.

JACK PERFECTLY ILLUSTRATED A TEAM THAT I'D BEEN *LONGING* TO WRITE ABOUT. HEROES WHO WERE *LESS THAN PERFECT.*

HEROES WHO DIDN'T ALWAYS GET ALONG WITH ONE ANOTHER, BUT HEROES WHO COULD BE *COUNTED ON* WHEN THE CHIPS WERE DOWN.

AND EVEN *BEFORE* THE SALES RESULTS WERE IN, WE KNEW WE HAD A *HIT* BECAUSE OF THE *MASSIVE AMOUNT OF...*

...FAN MAIL.

WE WERE *SWAMPED* WITH IT, AND IT JUST KEPT *GROWING* WITH EACH NEW ISSUE.

THAT'S WHY I CREATED THE LETTERS PAGES AND *STAN'S SOAPBOX.*

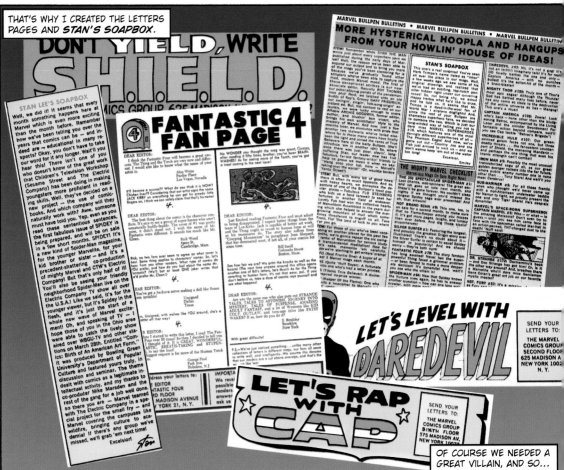

OF COURSE WE NEEDED A GREAT VILLAIN, AND SO...

NO! NOT *THAT* ONE!

THAAAAT'S BETTER.

IN *THE HUNCHBACK OF NOTRE DAME*, EVERYBODY ROOTS FOR *QUASIMODO*, JUST LIKE *THE THING* GETS THE MOST FAN MAIL IN THE *FANTASTIC FOUR*.

SO I WAS THINKING, WHAT IF HE COULD *CHANGE* BACK AND FORTH? A MONSTER WITH A *SECRET IDENTITY*.

YOU *KNOW*...

...LIKE *DR. JEKYLL*...

...AND *MR. HYDE*.

SO WE'LL START WITH THIS *GUY*. WE'LL CALL HIM *BRUCE BANNER.*

ANOTHER ALLITERATIVE NAME.

RIGHT, BECAUSE AGAIN, THAT'S *SO MUCH EASIER* TO REMEMBER!

YEAH, EXCEPT THAT WHEN HE GUEST-STARRED IN *FF* #25, I HAD HIM REFER TO HIMSELF AS *"BOB BANNER."*

SO A FEW ISSUES LATER IN THE *FF* LETTERS PAGE, I DECLARED HIS NAME WAS HENCEFORTH *"ROBERT* BRUCE BANNER."

IT WAS THE EASY WAY OUT!

I'LL HAVE HIM GET HIT BY THE RAYS OF A *GAMMA RAY BOMB!*

NO IDEA. BUT YOU'VE GOTTA ADMIT THEY *SOUND* GOOD.

WHAT ARE *GAMMA* RAYS?

AND THE RAYS TURN HIM *INTO...*

INTO *WHAT*? WHAT'S THE MONSTER'S *NAME*?

WHERE ARE YOU GOING?

TO GET A *THESAURUS!*

OKAY! GOT IT! WE'LL CALL HIM...

SHEEESH.

DESPITE **MARTIN**'S LACK OF ENDORSEMENT, THE **HULK** MADE HIS DEBUT IN MAY OF **1962**.

INITIALLY HIS SKIN WAS **GRAY**, BUT THE PRINTER HAD TROUBLE MAKING IT A **CONSISTENT** SHADE.

SO AS OF ISSUE #2, WITH **NO EXPLANATION**, HE TURNED **GREEN**. AND THAT'S THE COLOR HE STAYED...

...AT LEAST UNTIL HE TURNED **RED**, BUT THAT'S A WHOLE **'NOTHER** STORY.

AND THEN I CAME UP WITH **ANOTHER** IDEA.

IT'S THE *WORST* IDEA I'VE *EVER* HEARD! FOR STARTERS, YOU *CAN'T* HAVE A SUPERHERO BE A *TEENAGER*. TEENAGERS ARE *SIDEKICKS*.

ALSO, HE CAN'T HAVE TONS OF *PERSONAL PROBLEMS*. YOU'RE DESCRIBING A *COMEDY CHARACTER*, NOT A *HERO*.

HEROES ARE TOO BUSY FIGHTING *EVIL* TO DEAL WITH PERSONAL STUFF.

AND THE *NAME*--!

WHAT'S WRONG WITH CALLING HIM *SPIDER-MAN*?!

DON'T YOU REALIZE THAT PEOPLE *HATE* SPIDERS?

TELL ME YOU WERE *JOKING* AND WE'LL STILL BE FRIENDS.

OKAY, BUT WE'RE CANCELING *AMAZING ADULT FANTASY*. CAN I DROP THE *SPIDER-MAN* STORY IN ITS FINAL ISSUE?

WE'RE KILLING THE BOOK ANYWAY, SO *WHO CARES?*

A MONTH LATER...

STAN! DID YOU SEE THESE NUMBERS?

THE NUMBERS ON *AMAZING FANTASY* #15 WERE *HUGE*! THIS MAY BE THE *BEST-SELLING* COMICBOOK OF THE DECADE!

GLAD TO HEAR IT.

YOU KNOW THAT *SPIDER-MAN* IDEA OF YOURS THAT WE LIKED SO MUCH? WHY DON'T WE TURN IT INTO A SERIES?

THAT IS A GREAT IDEA, *MARTIN*. WE'LL GET RIGHT ON IT.

OH WELL, HE WAS THE BOSS. WHAT COULD I SAY?

SO THAT'S HOW *SPIDER-MAN* WAS CREATED.

SO THEN I THOUGHT I'D LIKE TO CREATE A HERO *EVEN MORE* POWERFUL THAN THE *HULK.*

BUT *HOW* COULD I DO IT? HOW COULD *ANY* HUMAN BE *STRONGER* THAN OL' GREENSKIN?

aaaaaaaaah

THEN I THOUGHT:

DON'T MAKE HIM A HUMAN!

MAKE HIM A *GOD!*

BUT MOST PEOPLE WERE ALREADY FAMILIAR WITH THE GREEK AND ROMAN GODS.

WHAT COULD I DO THAT WAS *DIFFERENT?*

I'VE *GOT IT! NORSE* GODS!

LOOKING LIKE *VIKINGS* OF OLD WITH FLOWING BEARDS, HORNED HELMETS, AND BATTLE CLUBS.

AND WHO WAS THE MOST *DRAMATIC* AND *HEROIC* NORSE GOD OF THEM ALL?

I WROTE AN OUTLINE FOR THE FIRST ISSUE AND THEN TURNED IT OVER TO MY BROTHER, LARRY LIEBER.
12¢
JOURNEY INTO
MYSTERY
APPROVED BY THE COMICS CODE AUTHORITY
MC
83 AUG.
INTRODUCING... THE MIGHTY THOR!
THE MOST EXCITING SUPER-HERO OF ALL TIME!!
HE SCRIPTED IT OVER PENCILS THAT WERE DRAWN BY JACK KIRBY.
BEGIN THE SAGA OF THOR IN THIS ISSUE!
BUT YOU KNOW WHAT? SINCE WE'RE TALKING ABOUT LARRY...

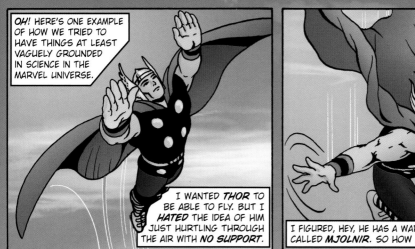

OH! HERE'S ONE EXAMPLE OF HOW WE TRIED TO HAVE THINGS AT LEAST VAGUELY GROUNDED IN SCIENCE IN THE MARVEL UNIVERSE.

I WANTED *THOR* TO BE ABLE TO FLY. BUT I *HATED* THE IDEA OF HIM JUST HURTLING THROUGH THE AIR WITH *NO SUPPORT.*

I FIGURED, HEY, HE HAS A WAR HAMMER CALLED *MJOLNIR.* SO HOW ABOUT...

...HE WILL HAVE THAT *HAMMER* WITH HIM. AND WHEN HE WANTS TO FLY...

...HE'LL *WHIRL* IT AROUND HIS HEAD REALLY FAST. AND THEN HE'LL *THROW* IT...

...AND SINCE HE'S *ATTACHED* TO IT BY THE THONG AROUND HIS WRIST--WHEN THE HAMMER GOES FLYING, IT'LL *TAKE HIM WITH IT!*

TO THIS DAY I DON'T KNOW WHY *NASA* HASN'T INVITED ME TO JOIN THEIR SCIENCE TEAM.

SO HERE WE HAD FLYING, FLAMING TEENAGERS, GREEN MONSTERS, GODS, SPIDER-MEN...

WHAT COULD I DO NEXT THAT WOULD BE *DIFFERENT*?

AS IT TURNED OUT, THE ANSWER LAY IN THE PAGES OF *TALES TO ASTONISH* #27...

IND.

TALES TO ASTONISH

APPROVED BY THE COMICS CODE AUTHORITY

27 JAN.

10¢

LET ME TELL YOU, WHILE I STILL CAN, HOW IT HAPPENED... FOR I WAS

"THE MAN IN THE ANT HILL!"

THERE WAS A STORY TITLED "THE MAN IN THE ANT HILL," WRITTEN BY *LARRY* AND ME.

SAVE ME, SOMEBODY, SAVE ME!! DON'T LET THEM DRAG ME THERE! NOT ≡GASP≡ INTO THE ANT HILL!!

THE STORY INTRODUCED *DR. HENRY PYM*, A BRILLIANT SCIENTIST WHO INVENTED A SHRINKING FORMULA.

AS SUCH GUYS ARE WONT TO DO, HE TESTED IT ON *HIMSELF*.

HE WOUND UP NEARLY GETTING HIMSELF KILLED.

HE MADE IT BACK TO HIS LAB, RESTORED HIS HEIGHT, AND POURED OUT THE SERUMS.

BUT YOU CAN'T KEEP A GOOD SCIENTIST, OR COMICBOOK CHARACTER, DOWN. A FEW MONTHS LATER, *HENRY PYM* HAD CREATED A HELMET THAT ENABLED HIM TO COMMUNICATE WITH ANTS...

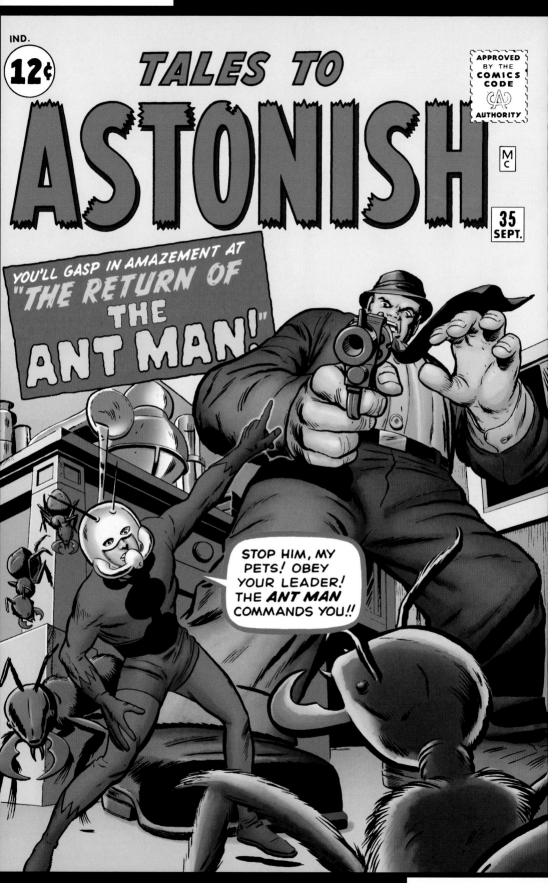

THE *VIETNAM WAR*, FOR EXAMPLE.

WE HAD JUST GOTTEN OUT OF *KOREA* ONLY A FEW YEARS EARLIER...

...AND PROTESTERS WERE ALREADY GEARING UP TO OPPOSE *VIETNAM*, SOMETHING THAT WOULD SWALLOW MUCH OF THE LATTER PART OF THE DECADE.

AND IF THERE IS ONE TYPE OF PERSON KIDS HAVE *NO* PATIENCE FOR, IT IS MILITARY INDUSTRIALISTS.

SO NATURALLY...

YOU WANT YOUR *NEXT* HERO TO BE A *MILITARY INDUSTRIALIST?*

EXACTLY!

HE'LL BE A TYCOON WHO INVENTS AND MANUFACTURES WEAPONS AND MUNITIONS AND *SELLS* THEM TO THE MILITARY!

HE'LL BE A *BILLIONAIRE INDUSTRIALIST*, THE *QUINTESSENTIAL CAPITALIST*, AND I'LL TRY TO FIND A WAY TO MAKE OUR READERS *LIKE* HIM!

YOU'RE CRAZY.

OF *COURSE* HE SAID THAT.

BUT HE DIDN'T SAY *"NO."* SO I WORKED WITH MY OLD FRIEND, ARTIST *DON HECK*...

OR MARVEL MOVIE STUDIOS...
IND.

12¢

APPROVED BY THE COMICS CODE AUTHORITY

SUSPENSE

MC

39 MAR.

WHO? OR WHAT, IS THE NEWEST, MOST BREATH-TAKING, MOST SENSATIONAL SUPER HERO OF ALL...?

"IRON MAN!"

...IN A FILM THAT WOULD TAKE IN MORE THAN *$585 MILLION* AT THE BOX OFFICE.

CONQUERS!

WHO?

WHO?

WHO?

NOT BAD FOR A GUY MY BOSS EXPECTED THE TEENS TO *HATE*.

FROM THE TALENTED BULLPEN WHERE THE FANTASTIC FOUR, SPIDER-MAN, THOR AND YOUR OTHER FAVORITE SUPER HEROES WERE BORN!

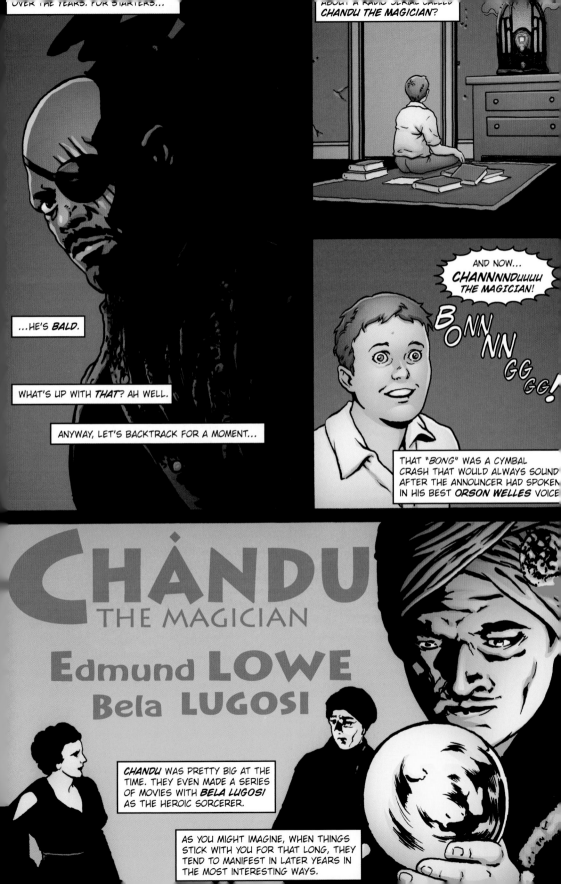

...HE'S **BALD**.

WHAT'S UP WITH *THAT*? AH WELL.

ANYWAY, LET'S BACKTRACK FOR A MOMENT...

AND NOW... *CHANNNNDuuuu THE MAGICIAN!*

BONN NN GG GG!

THAT "*BONG*" WAS A CYMBAL CRASH THAT WOULD ALWAYS SOUND AFTER THE ANNOUNCER HAD SPOKEN IN HIS BEST *ORSON WELLES* VOICE

CHÁNDU
THE MAGICIAN
Edmund LOWE
Bela LUGOSI

CHANDU WAS PRETTY BIG AT THE TIME. THEY EVEN MADE A SERIES OF MOVIES WITH *BELA LUGOSI* AS THE HEROIC SORCERER.

AS YOU MIGHT IMAGINE, WHEN THINGS STICK WITH YOU FOR THAT LONG, THEY TEND TO MANIFEST IN LATER YEARS IN THE MOST INTERESTING WAYS.

DOC STRANGE IS ACTUALLY A POPULAR SUBJECT ON COLLEGE CAMPUSES. AND, MAN, WERE WE POPULAR ON THOSE.

IT'S AMAZING HOW I HAD BEEN CONCERNED ABOUT COMICS BEING STRICTLY CHILDREN'S MATERIAL, AND IN JUST A FEW YEARS WE WERE HUGE ON CAMPUSES.

I'VE PROBABLY LECTURED AT MORE COLLEGES THAN ANYONE ELSE I CAN THINK OF.

IT'S THE GREATEST WAY TO STAY IN TOUCH WITH THE INTELLIGENT ADULT FANS THAT I AM SO PROUD OF.

AND VERY OFTEN I WAS EVEN PAID...

THEY PAY YOU FOR ONE SPEECH, BUT YOU WIND UP MAKING THREE OR FOUR.

FIRST, THERE'S...

SPEECH #1

LUGGAGE COLLECTION

STAN LEE!

HOW WAS YOUR TRIP, MR. LEE?

UNEVENTFUL, WHICH IS JUST HOW YOU WANT PLANE TRIPS TO BE.

CAN I HELP YOU WITH YOUR BAG?

SURE!

WE HAVE A CAR RIGHT OUTSIDE.

GOOD TO HEAR.

STAN, MY FRAT BROTHERS AND I HAVE BEEN WONDERING...

IS IT TRUE THAT YOU BASED *DR. STRANGE*'S SPELLS ON THE INCANTATIONS OF THE ANCIENT DRUIDS?

WELL, I--

DON'T BE *RIDICULOUS!* I'VE BEEN RESEARCHING THIS--

OW!

AND IT'S *OBVIOUS* HE BASES THEM ON A COMBINATION OF THE *ROSETTA STONE* AND THE *DEAD SEA SCROLLS!*

WHAT THE *HELL* ARE YOU *TALKING ABOUT?!*

SPEECH #1 IS THE TYPICAL Q&A I WIND UP IN THE MIDDLE OF FROM THE STUDENTS WHO PICK ME UP.

THAT TAKES US TO...

NATURALLY, I SHOWED UP WEARING JEANS AND A SLOPPY SHIRT, LIKE THE GUYS AT *BARD*.

YOU CAN *GUESS* HOW EVERYONE ELSE WAS ATTIRED.

MORE WINE, SIR?

There isn't enough wine in the world to quench my embarrassment.

SPEECH #3

SO TELL ME, *MR. LEE*: WHAT IS IT LIKE PUBLISHING *SUPERMAN*?

* sigh *

AND THEN, OF COURSE... THE TRIP BACK.

SPEECH #4

IT'S *OBVIOUS* THAT THE *X-MEN* ARE SUPPOSED TO BE SYNONYMOUS WITH *GAYS*...

NO, THEY'RE *NOT!* IT'S *CLEARLY* ABOUT *RACISM!* RIGHT, *STAN*?

WELL, SINCE YOU ASKED...

NO, *STAN*, IT'S OKAY, I'VE GOT THIS COVERED.

THEY'RE YOUNGSTERS WHO REALIZE WHEN THEY'RE *TEENS* THAT THEY'RE *DIFFERENT*? HOW GAY IS THAT?

* sigh *

...WE'LL HAVE A GROUP OF TEENAGERS WHO WERE SIMPLY *BORN* WITH THEIR POWERS.

AND WE CAN HAVE AS *MANY* AS WE WANT BECAUSE NATURE DOESN'T LIMIT THE NUMBER OF MUTATIONS.

AND WE'LL CALL IT...

THE *MUTANTS!*

the *MUTANTS*

I LIKE THE CONCEPT, BUT THE *TITLE'S* TERRIBLE.

WHY?

MOST READERS WON'T KNOW WHAT A *MUTANT* IS.

COME UP WITH SOMETHING ELSE.

the *MUTA*

WELL... THEY'RE HEROES WITH *EXTRA* POWERS.

THEIR MENTOR IS A GUY NAMED *PROFESSOR XAVIER.*

SO HOW ABOUT WE CALL THEM...

THE STRANGEST SUPER-HEROES OF ALL!

1 SEPT.

IND.

APPROVED BY THE COMICS CODE AUTHORITY

The X-MEN

MARVEL COMICS GROUP 12¢

IN THE SENSATIONAL FANTASTIC FOUR STYLE!

OF COURSE, THAT **NEVER** REALLY MADE ANY SENSE.

IF THE READERS DIDN'T KNOW WHAT A MUTANT WAS, HOW WOULD THEY KNOW WHAT AN **X-MAN** WAS?

X-MEN VERSUS **MAGNETO** EARTH'S MOST POWERFUL SUPER VILLAIN!!

BUT IT KEPT **MARTIN** HAPPY, SO I FIGURED, THE HECK WITH IT.

SINCE THEN, OF COURSE...

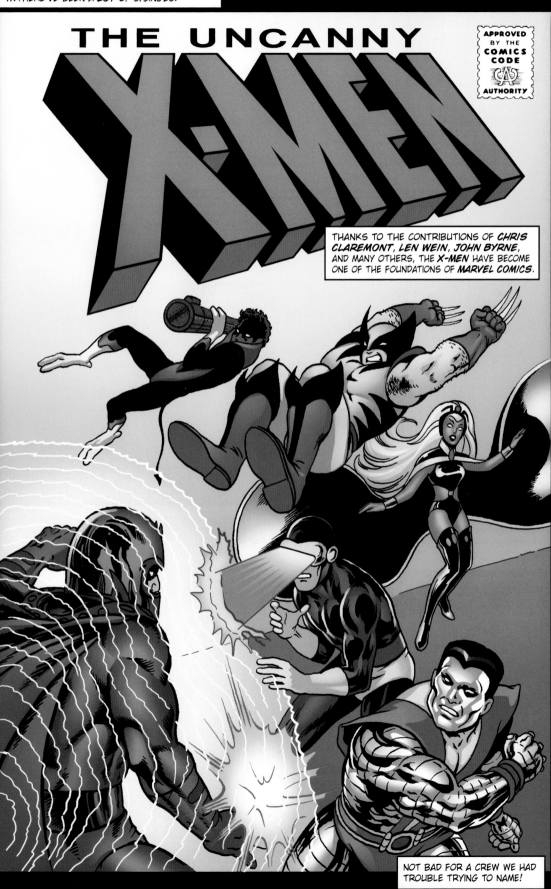

OUR SALES ARE BETTER THAN EVER, *MARTIN!* YOU'VE GOTTA ADMIT, EVERYTHING'S GOING *GREAT!* MY GUYS ARE TURNING OUT--

MY GUYS, *STAN. I'M* THE ONE WHO *PAYS* THEM.

YEAH, AND YOU PAY THEM *WAY LESS* THAN THE EDITORS AND WRITERS OF YOUR MOVIE AND MEN'S MAGAZINES.

Y'KNOW WHY? BECAUSE *THOSE* MAGS ARE ON A *HIGHER* CULTURAL PLATEAU THAN OUR *COMIC-BOOKS.*

IN FACT, IF I RAISED THE PRICE ON THE COMICS A FEW *PENNIES,* I'D MAKE MORE MONEY BY THAT *ONE DECISION...*

...THAN BY *ALL* THE WORK YOU DO IN A *YEAR.*

YOU REMEMBER THAT.

AS PARANOID AS IT SOUNDED, I WAS STARTING TO THINK OUR MILLIONAIRE BOSS SOMEHOW RESENTED OUR SUCCESS.

MR. *LEE!* WE HAD AN INTERVIEW SCHEDULED?

Martin odman

IT MIGHT'VE BEEN BECAUSE I WAS SEEN BY REPORTERS AS THE FACE OF THE COMPANY, AND IT MADE *MARTIN* JEALOUS.

LUCKILY THERE WAS TOO MUCH HAPPENING, TOO MUCH TO DO, FOR ME TO DWELL ON *MARTIN'S* ATTITUDE FOR LONG.

STAN?

AH, *FABULOUS FLO STEINBERG!* MY INTREPID ASSISTANT/ RECEPTIONIST/ GAL FRIDAY!

WHY DO YOU ALWAYS SOUND LIKE YOU'RE TALKING TO SOMEONE ELSE?

DRAMATIC LICENSE. DON'T WORRY ABOUT IT. WHAT'S UP?

COUPLE OF THINGS. I WAS JUST WONDERING ABOUT THIS WORD YOU STARTED USING IN THE SOAPBOX.

WHAT WORD?

EXCELSIOR.

NO, NO! IT'S NOT *"EXCELSIOR."* IT'S PRONOUNCED...

Ex-CEL-si-or!

THAT'S THE STUFF WE USE TO PACK THINGS IN BOXES.

NO, IT'S *LATIN!* IT MEANS *"TO THE HIGHEST!"*

Okay, whatever.

ALSO, WE SHOULD DO SOMETHING ABOUT THE FAN MAIL.

LIKE HERE, WHEN YOU HAD THE CONTEST CHALLENGING PEOPLE TO PROVE THAT *NAMOR* WAS A MUTANT.

YEAH! WE GOT *GREAT LETTERS* ABOUT THAT.

YES, BUT THEY WANT PRIZES FOR IT.

I TOLD THEM! I SAID WE WERE GIVING OUT *NO* PRIZES, AND SINCE *NOBODY* GOT A PRIZE, IT WOULD BE A CONTEST WITH *NO LOSERS.*

BUT THEY WANT PRIZES ANYWAY.

HMM, LET ME THINK.

WHEN IS A PRIZE NOT A PRIZE?

GOT IT.

GOT *WHAT?*

WE'LL GIVE THEM A *PRIZE.*

RIGHT. WE SEND IT IN A *SPECIAL* ENVELOPE.

BUT YOU SAID YOU DIDN'T WANT TO.

STAN, WE DON'T HAVE A BUDGET TO PUT PRIZES IN ENVELOPES.

EXACTLY WHAT?

EXACTLY!

WHERE ARE OUR SCRIPTS?

SCRIPTS? WE DON'T NEED SCRIPTS!

WHATTAYA MEAN, WE DON'T NEED SCRIPTS?!

WE'LL JUST AD-LIB FOR FIVE MINUTES. IT'LL BE GREAT!

CAN I PLAY MY HARMONICA INSTEAD OF TALK?

YOU'RE ADORABLE ARTIE SIMEK! YOU CAN DO WHATEVER YOU WANT!

OKAY OUT THERE IN MARVEL LAND! FACE FRONT! THIS IS STAN LEE SPEAKING, AND YOU PROBABLY HAVE NEVER HEARD A RECORD LIKE THIS BEFORE...

...BECAUSE NO ONE WOULD BE NUTTY ENOUGH TO MAKE ONE WITH A BUNCH OF OFFBEAT ARTISTS, SO ANYTHING IS LIKELY TO HAPPEN.

SAY, WHO MADE YOU A DISC JOCKEY, LEE?

WELL, WELL, JOLLY JACK KIRBY! SAY A FEW WORDS TO THE FANS, JACK.

OKAY: A FEW WORDS.

LOOK, PAL, I'LL TAKE CARE OF THE HUMOR AROUND HERE.

HUMOR! YOU'VE BEEN USING THE SAME GAGS OVER AND OVER FOR YEARS!

BY THE WAY, *JACK:* READERS HAVE BEEN *COMPLAINING* ABOUT SUE STORM'S *HAIRDO* AGAIN.

WHAT AM *I*, HER *HAIRDRESSER*? NEXT TIME, I'LL DRAW HER *BALD-HEADED!*

STAN! DO YOU HAVE A FEW MINUTES?

FOR OUR *FABULOUS GAL FRIDAY*? *SURE.* SAY HELLO TO THE FANS, *FLO STEINBERG.*

HELLO, FANS, IT'S VERY NICE TO MEET YOU. AS MARVEL'S CORRESPONDING SECRETARY, I FEEL I *KNOW* MOST OF YOU FROM YOUR LETTERS.

AND *SOL BRODSKY* WANTS TO SAY A FEW WORDS.

SOL BRODSKY? WHO'S *HE*?

STAN, THE FANS KNOW YOU HAVE A TERRIBLE MEMORY AS PROVEN BY ALL THE *MISTAKES* YOU MAKE, BUT *THIS IS RIDICULOUS.*

HE'S BEEN YOUR ASSOCIATE FOR *YEARS!*

REALLY? WE OUGHTA START *PAYING HIM* ONE OF THESE DAYS.

I'VE BEEN MEANING TO TALK TO YOU ABOUT THAT. AND HOW COME *I* DON'T GET MY NAME *PLASTERED ALL OVER THE MAGS* LIKE *YOU DO?!*

BECAUSE I CAN'T *SPELL* IT, THAT'S WHY.

WELL, AS LONG AS YOU'VE GOT A GOOD REASON.

SAY, WHAT'S ALL THAT *COMMOTION* OUT THERE, *SOL?*

WHY, IT'S *SHY STEVE DITKO.*

WE WANTED HIM ON THIS RECORDING BUT HE'S GOT MIKE FRIGHT.

WHOOPS! THERE HE *GOES!*

OUT THE *WINDOW AGAIN?* YOU KNOW, I'M STARTING TO THINK HE *IS SPIDER-MAN.*

YOU MEAN HE *ISN'T?*

WHO *SAID* THAT?

JUST THAT LOVABLE OLD LETTERER: *ME.*

WHY, IT'S *ADORABLE ARTIE SIMEK.* WHAT BROUGHT YOU HERE?

THE *SUBWAY.*

STAN, THIS IS THE MOST *CONFUSED* RECORD I EVER *HEARD.*

GREAT, SOL! JUST WHAT WE *WANT!*

IF IT WERE *ANYTHING* ELSE, IT WOULDN'T BE THE *NUTTY MARVEL BULLPEN!*

WE DON'T HAVE TIME FOR *GEORGE BELL* AND *VINCE COLLETTA* AND *LARRY LIEBER* AND *BOB POWELL*...

THAT'S *GREAT!* IF WE EVER FORM ANOTHER CLUB, WE'LL HAVE SOMETHING *NEW* TO OFFER! MORE VOICES THAT HAVEN'T BEEN *HEARD* YET!

'NUFF SAID, *SOL!* NOW, LET'S ALL GET BACK TO WORK IN THE BULLPEN.

AND AS FOR *YOU,* MARVELOUS MERRY MARCHERS, WELCOME...

...FROM ALL OF *US* TO ALL OF *YOU!*

IF YOU WANT TO KNOW HOW GLAD WE ARE TO HAVE YOU WITH US, JUST YOU LISTEN:

OKAY! LET 'EM *HEAR* IT, GANG!

WAAAAAA-HOOOOo!!!!

> NOBODY HAD EVER GOTTEN ANYTHING LIKE THAT BEFORE, WHERE THEY ACTUALLY HEARD THE VOICES OF THE PEOPLE WHOSE STORIES THEY HAD BEEN READING.

THE VOICES OF MARVEL

A SPECIALLY RECORDED MESSAGE TO YOU FROM YOUR BULLPEN BUDDIES

SCREAM ALONG WITH MARVEL

WHO SAYS THIS ISN'T THE MARVEL AGE OF RIOTOUS RECORDINGS?

WELCOME TO THE ANCIENT AND HONORABLE ORDER OF

The Merry Marvel Marching Society

be it known

_____
authorized signature

is a charter member in good standing of

The Merry Marvel Marching Society

And is thereby entitled to the adulation and admiration of all lesser mortals!

Benj. J. Grimm
GRAND MARSHAL (pro tem)

these privileges are non-transferable

I BELONG

THE MERRY MARVEL MARCHING SOCIETY

Congratulations, favored one!

...For having the wisdom and wit to become

> IT'S A WONDER THEY DIDN'T CANCEL THEIR SUBSCRIPTIONS ON THE SPOT!

Your name has been ceremoniously entered in our log book, and your dollar has been avariciously deposited in our treasury!

From this day forth, you will stand a little straighter, speak a little wiser, and walk a little prouder. You've made the scene! You're in! You've joined the winning team!

such triumph comes responsibility. You must use your valued member-
rileges judiciously. You must be true to the Marvel Code of Ethics: Be
ant towards those who have shunned our ranks, for they know not what
issing. Be not hostile towards unbelievers who march with others, for
ore to be pitied than scorned. Be not intolerant of Marvel-defamers, for
hall someday see the light. And, above all, be not forgetful that you have
r bullpen buddy. Henceforth, you shall never march alone!

elcome you to the fold with this sagacious admonition—FACE FRONT!
of us now!

'Nuff said!

The Bullpen Gang

THE M.M.M.S. WANTS YOU!

> BUT IT WAS A HUGE HIT, AND I FELT THAT IT WOULD RUN FOR DECADES! MAYBE FOREVER!

FIVE YEARS LATER...

Martin Goodman

SHUT DOWN THE FAN CLUB?!? *WHY?!!*

SHOUTING MY OWN WORDS BACK AT ME ISN'T THE BEST WAY TO CONDUCT THIS MEETING.

BUT *WHY,* *MARTIN?* IT'S *SUCCESSFUL!*

BECAUSE IT'S TOO *EXPENSIVE* FOR THE COMPANY TO SERVICE.

IT COSTS TOO MUCH MONEY TO SEND OUT ALL THE STUFF.

BUT IT'S *GREAT PUBLIC RELATIONS!* THE FANS *LOVE IT!*

WE DON'T NEED GREAT PUBLIC RELATIONS. WE *NEED* GREAT SALES.

WE'RE *GETTING* GREAT SALES!

SO THEN WE'RE COVERED.

LET'S GO OVER THIS AGAIN...

NO, *STAN,* LET'S NOT. IT'S DONE.

PULL THE PLUG ON THE *M.M.M.S.*

AND SO THAT WAS IT.

EXCEPT I WAITED A FEW YEARS UNTIL *MARTIN* WASN'T LOOKING AND...

WELL, REMEMBER WHEN I MENTIONED *JIM STERANKO* EARLIER...?

GREAT SEEING YOU AS ALWAYS, *JIM!* SO WHAT'S UP?

NOTHING MUCH. JUST WANTED TO CHAT WITH YOU ABOUT THE CURRENT COMICS SCENE.

HOW'S IT GOING WITH YOU AND THE FANS?

IT'S GOING *GREAT*, ALTHOUGH...

ALTHOUGH WHAT?

I MISS OUR FAN CLUB. THAT WAS SUCH A GREAT CONNECTION TO THE FANS.

AW, MAN, YEAH. I REMEMBER THE OLD DAYS OF RADIO SHOWS WITH THE CLUBS AND SUPER-PREMIUMS.

YOU KNOW WHAT YOU SHOULD HAVE?

A *FAN* MAGAZINE.

IF *YOU* PUBLISH IT...

YOU'LL EDIT IT?

I'M A FRIEND OF OL' MARVEL. I'M HERE FOR YOU.

Y'KNOW, THAT'S NOT A BAD TITLE.

WHAT, "FRIENDS OF OLD MARVEL"? IT'S TOO LONG.

SO WE *SHORTEN* IT!

...THE WHITE HOUSE. DURING THE *JIMMY CARTER* ERA, A GROUP OF US FROM *MARVEL COMICS* WAS INVITED.

I THINK THEY WANTED TO HAVE *CAPTAIN AMERICA* AS A SYMBOL OF ENVIRONMENTALISM OR SOME SUCH.

A FEW OF US WENT THERE, INCLUDING SEVERAL ACTORS DRESSED AS OUR CHARACTERS.

IT SEEMED HARMLESS ENOUGH.

THE THING WAS, *PRESIDENT CARTER* HIMSELF WASN'T THERE. SO WE WERE SUPPOSED TO MEET HIS WIFE, *ROSALYNN*, AND DAUGHTER, *AMY*.

SO *ROSALYNN* AND *AMY* COME OUT THE FRONT DOOR OF THE WHITE HOUSE.

AND SUDDENLY THE *IDIOT* DRESSED AS THE *GREEN GOBLIN* DECIDES TO ACT IN CHARACTER, APPARENTLY FORGETTING WHERE HE WAS.

I'M GOING TO GETCHA, LITTLE GIRL!!

HE SCARED LITTLE **AMY CARTER**, BUT THAT WASN'T THE **MAIN** PROBLEM.

THE **MAIN** PROBLEM WAS...

...IN SECONDS SHE WAS SURROUNDED BY THE SECRET SERVICE!

AND ALL THEY SAW WAS A CRAZY MAN THREATENING THE DAUGHTER OF THE **PRESIDENT OF THE UNITED STATES!**

I SEE THEM ALL GOING FOR THEIR **GUNS!**

OKAY, **OKAY! HOLD ON!**

GUYS, HE'S **NOT A THREAT!**

I AM THE **GREEN GOBLIN!**

YOU'LL BE A **DEAD** GOBLIN IF YOU DON'T **SHADDUP!** THOSE ARE SECRET SERVICE MEN AND THEIR GUNS ARE **REAL!**

UH-OH.

YEAH, YOU **BET** "UH-OH"!

I THINK I'LL JUST STAND OVER HERE.

GOOD IDEA.

Sheeesh.

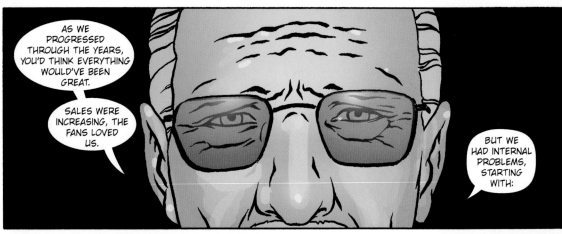

AS WE PROGRESSED THROUGH THE YEARS, YOU'D THINK EVERYTHING WOULD'VE BEEN GREAT.

SALES WERE INCREASING, THE FANS LOVED US.

BUT WE HAD INTERNAL PROBLEMS, STARTING WITH:

STEVE DITKO.

HE JUST DIDN'T SEEM HAPPY WORKING WITH ME ANYMORE.

I WAS NEVER SURE WHAT BOTHERED HIM BUT I COULD TELL HE WAS DISSATISFIED.

WHATEVER THE REASON, THERE WAS NO LONGER ANY WARMTH TO OUR RELATIONSHIP.

AS I LOOK BACK ON THAT TIME, I FEEL THAT STEVE MAY HAVE FELT SOMEHOW SLIGHTED.

HE WANTED TO BE KNOWN AS SPIDER-MAN'S CO-CREATOR.

AND THAT WAS OKAY WITH ME. I STARTED CALLING ALL THE ARTISTS WHO DID A FIRST ISSUE WITH ME MY CO-CREATORS.

BUT DESPITE THAT, BY 1966, I'M SORRY TO SAY, HE WAS GONE.

FORTUNATELY, WE HAD A TOPFLIGHT TALENT IN THE PERSON OF *JOHN ROMITA* TO TAKE OVER.

HE MANAGED TO DRAW IN *STEVE'S* STYLE UNTIL, LITTLE BY LITTLE, HE EVOLVED INTO HIS OWN *GREAT* STYLE.

AND *BOY*, COULD HE DRAW *FEMALES!*

PETER PARKER, I'D LIKE YOU TO MEET MY *NIECE...*

YOU MEAN... *THAT'S* MARY JANE..?!!

FACE IT, TIGER...

YOU JUST HIT THE *JACKPOT!*

HMMM. SHE REMINDS ME OF *JOANIE* A LITTLE BIT.

NEXT: "THE RHINO ON THE RAMPAGE!" PLUS: A SWINGIN' SURPRISE OR TWO! 'NUFF SAID!

JOHN WAS THE ANCHOR OF OUR ART STAFF. WHATEVER HAD TO BE DRAWN HE DREW IT BEAUTIFULLY, QUICKLY, AND *PERFECTLY.* HE'S SIMPLY A GREAT *ARTIST* AND A GREAT *GUY.*

ONE THING I'VE ALWAYS REGRETTED-- I'D FREQUENTLY ASKED *JACK* TO TAKE ON THE *ART DIRECTOR* JOB AT *MARVEL*, SINCE WE'D'VE BEEN WORKING *TOGETHER* ON *EVERYTHING*.

BUT HE NEVER ACCEPTED THE OFFER. HE PREFERRED TO REMAIN FREELANCE. WHICH DISAPPOINTED ME BECAUSE HE'D HAVE BEEN A *GREAT* ARTIST/ART DIRECTOR.

WHERE'S his NOSE?

WHAT?

SHOULDN'T IRON MAN HAVE A NOSE?

OKAY, STAN. SURE!

GEORGE! STAN wants IRON MAN to have a NOSE.

THAT WAS GEORGE TUSKA. LONGTIME GREAT MARVEL ARTIST WHO HAD ALSO DRAWN CAPTAIN MARVEL.

WHAT? JEEZ. I'LL GET FRIEDRICH ON THE PHONE.

MIKE FRIEDRICH WAS A TERRIFIC WRITER WHO LATER WENT ON TO WRITE JLA AND ALSO CREATED STAR*REACH, ONE OF THE FIRST INDEPENDENT COMICS.

A NOSE?! WHAT THE HELL, TUSKA! ARE YOU SURE?

FINE. I'LL COME UP WITH SOMETHING.

THAT'S WHAT HE SAID.

IRON MAN #68

AND THEN...THE DRAMATIC RESULTS!

FORTUNATELY THE RAW MATERIALS ARE HERE AT MY FINGERTIPS...

I CAN EASILY MOLD A NEW MASK OUT OF REINFORCED STEEL MESH, LIKE THE REST OF MY ARMOR--

SO THAT I CAN MENTALLY COMMAND MY SUIT'S EQUIPMENT AND WEAPONRY! AND THIS TIME I'VE FASHIONED INCREASED-STRENGTH PLEXIGLASS-LIKE EYE- AND-MOUTH SHIELDS THAT WILL WITHSTAND THE DEEPEST OCEANS--

AND I'LL FINISH THE ARMOR'S CHANGES WITH A SLIGHTLY MOD-IFIED APPEARANCE... TO ALLOW A BIT MORE EXPRESSION TO SHOW--

ONE YEAR LATER...

UH... WHAT'S THIS?

WHAT'S *WHAT?*

WHY DOES *IRON MAN* HAVE A *NOSE* IN HIS ARMOR? IT LOOKS *RIDICULOUS.* HE SHOULDN'T HAVE THAT THERE.

WHAT THE HELL?!?

HE *ASKED* FOR THE NOSE! *YOU* TOLD ME THAT!

IT'S WHAT HE *SAID.*

I *KNOW!*

HE WANTS THE NOSE *GONE?!?* HE *ASKED* FOR THE NOSE!

I'M CALLING *LEN WEIN!!* HE'S THE *DAMN EDITOR!* LET *HIM* HANDLE THIS!

THEY SAID YOU *WANTED* A NOSE ON HIS MASK!

WHEN DID I SAY *THAT?!*

A *YEAR* AGO! YOU LOOKED AT A COVER AND SAID, "*WHERE'S HIS NOSE?*"

OH, FOR *CRYING OUT--*

I MEANT THAT THE HELMET LOOKED *SO TIGHT* ON HIS FACE THAT I WONDERED HOW *TONY STARK'S* NOSE *FIT* IN THERE!

I WANTED THE HELMET A LITTLE *BIGGER,* THAT'S *ALL!*

TAKE THE NOSE *OFF* THE HELMET.

BOY, *STAN* JUST *CANNOT* MAKE UP HIS MIND.

IT *WASN'T EASY* BEING EDITOR IN CHIEF.

THAT'S *HYSTERICAL!* "*IRON MAN'S NOSE*"?

WELL, IT'S MY FAULT. I'M OUT SO FREQUENTLY THESE DAYS THAT NO ONE HAS TIME TO DOUBLE-CHECK WITH ME.

SO INSTEAD OF ASKING, "*STAN,* WHAT DID YOU MEAN?" THEY JUST INTERPRET WHAT I SAY AND RUN WITH IT.

AND HOW ARE THINGS GOING?

WELL, BOB, YOU KNOW *MARTIN* SOLD THE COMPANY A WHILE BACK. TO *PERFECT FILM.*

IN FACT, THEY--

HEY, KID. YOU KNOW WHO YOU'VE BEEN WAITING ON THIS EVENING?

AW, *NOT AGAIN.*

I'M *BOB KANE!*

UH... *WHO?*

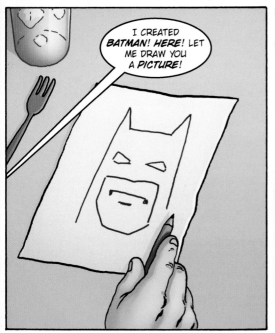

I CREATED *BATMAN! HERE!* LET ME DRAW YOU A *PICTURE!*

SURE, WE MAY HAVE BEEN IN COMPETITION, BUT I DID HAVE A FEW FRIENDS WHO WORKED FOR OUR *DISTINGUISHED COMPETITION.*

BOB KANE WAS PROBABLY THE MOST WELL-KNOWN.

WHILE **BOB** ENTERTAINED THE WAITER I THOUGHT BACK TO A MOMENT WITH **MARTIN GOODMAN** SHORTLY BEFORE HE LEFT **MARVEL**.

I'M GOING TO MAKE YOU A GIFT OF SOME **VALUABLE** WARRANTS.

WHAT ARE **THOSE**?

THEY'RE LIKE STOCK OPTIONS.

I FIGURED, THIS IS **GREAT**! WHAT A **NICE** THING FOR **MARTIN** TO DO.

MY POT OF GOLD HAD ARRIVED, AND I DIDN'T EVEN HAVE TO **ASK**!

PROBLEM IS, NOT ONLY WERE THE WARRANTS WORTHLESS...

HERE YOU GO!

THANKS. UH...

...BUT MARTIN NEVER EVEN **GAVE** THEM TO ME!

IS THIS **INSTEAD** OF A TIP?

EVENTUALLY, *PERFECT*'S STOCKHOLDERS AND BOARD OF DIRECTORS FORCED OUT THE COMPANY'S CHIEF EXEC, *MARTIN ACKERMAN*, AND REPLACED HIM WITH *SHELDON FEINBERG*.

PERFECT FILM

SHELDON WOUND UP CHANGING THE COMPANY'S NAME...

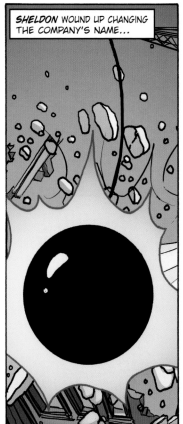

...TO *CADENCE INDUSTRIES*.

CADENCE INDUSTRIES

AND *MARVEL*'S NEW OWNERS HAD A PROPOSAL FOR ME.

PUBLISHER?! YOU WANT TO MAKE ME *PUBLISHER?!*

AT THAT POINT, COMPETITION REALLY HEATED UP BETWEEN US AND *DC COMICS*.

WE BASICALLY TRIED TO GRAB BIGGER SHARES OF THE MARKET BY CRANKING UP THE NUMBER OF TITLES WE PRODUCED.

THE RESULT WAS A LESSENING IN QUALITY AND TONS OF LATE-SHIPPING TITLES.

MEANWHILE, *MARTIN*, PARTLY--I THINK--OUT OF ANGER TOWARD ME, LEAPED BACK INTO COMICS PUBLISHING, REVIVING *ATLAS COMICS*.

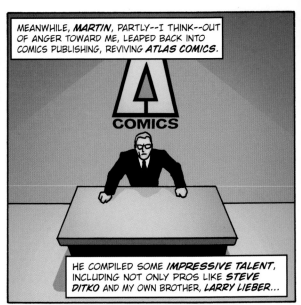

HE COMPILED SOME *IMPRESSIVE TALENT*, INCLUDING NOT ONLY PROS LIKE *STEVE DITKO* AND MY OWN BROTHER, *LARRY LIEBER*...

...BUT ALSO BIG NAMES SUCH AS *NEAL ADAMS* AND *WALT SIMONSON*.

HE PROMISED HIGHER PAGE RATES AND THAT HE WOULD EVEN RETURN THE ORIGINAL ARTWORK TO THEM, SOMETHING THAT WASN'T AN INDUSTRY PRACTICE.

OF COURSE, YEARS AGO, WHEN I WANTED TO RETURN ORIGINAL ARTWORK TO ALL ARTISTS...

...*MARTIN* REFUSED TO ALLOW ME TO DO SO!

ANYWAY, NEARLY A YEAR LATER, *ATLAS COMICS* HAD FOLDED AND I WAS HAPPILY HIRING BACK EVERYONE WHO HAD WORKED FOR THEM.

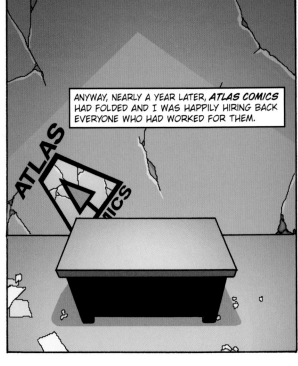

SO, NOW THAT I WAS PUBLISHER, I APPOINTED A TALENTED WRITER/EDITOR NAMED *ROY THOMAS* TO TAKE MY PLACE AS EDITOR IN CHIEF.

ROY HAD *TERRIFIC* INSTINCTS. FOR INSTANCE, A FEW YEARS EARLIER HE HAD MASTER-MINDED *MARVEL*'S ACQUIRING A NEW PROPERTY YOU MAY HAVE HEARD OF:

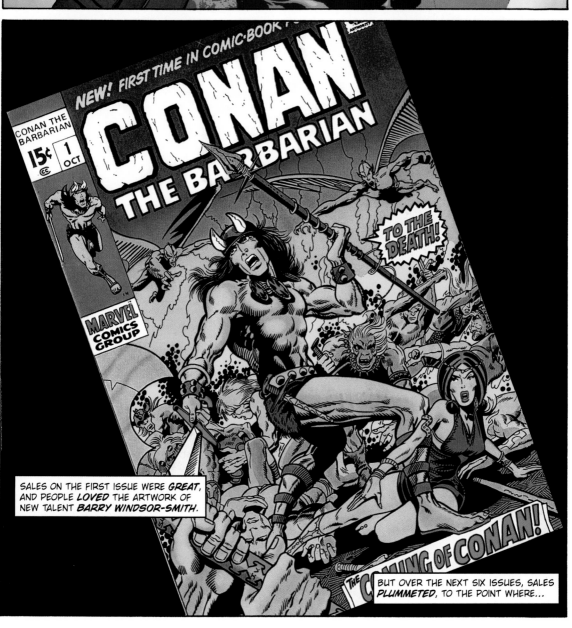

SALES ON THE FIRST ISSUE WERE *GREAT*, AND PEOPLE *LOVED* THE ARTWORK OF NEW TALENT *BARRY WINDSOR-SMITH*.

BUT OVER THE NEXT SIX ISSUES, SALES *PLUMMETED*, TO THE POINT WHERE...

YOU'RE **CANCELING IT?!** YOU **CAN'T** CANCEL IT!

BUT, **ROY,** LOOK AT THE **SALES!**

STICK WITH THE BOOK AND THEY'LL GO **UP!** I **SWEAR!**

IT'S NOT **JUST** THE SALES. I MEAN, WE SWITCHED FROM BIMONTHLY TO MONTHLY AND THE SALES DROPPED, BUT THAT'S NOT THE BIG THING.

IT'S **BARRY!** HIS ART IS **TERRIFIC!**

HOW IS **THAT** A PROBLEM?

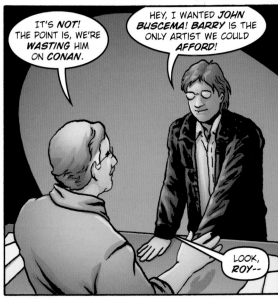

IT'S **NOT!** THE POINT IS, WE'RE **WASTING** HIM ON **CONAN.**

HEY, I WANTED **JOHN BUSCEMA! BARRY** IS THE ONLY ARTIST WE COULD **AFFORD!**

LOOK, **ROY--**

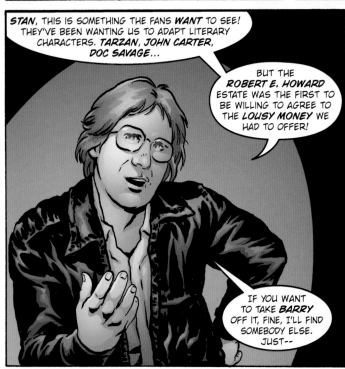

STAN, THIS IS SOMETHING THE FANS **WANT** TO SEE! THEY'VE BEEN WANTING US TO ADAPT LITERARY CHARACTERS. **TARZAN, JOHN CARTER, DOC SAVAGE...**

BUT THE **ROBERT E. HOWARD** ESTATE WAS THE FIRST TO BE WILLING TO AGREE TO THE **LOUSY MONEY** WE HAD TO OFFER!

IF YOU WANT TO TAKE **BARRY** OFF IT, FINE, I'LL FIND SOMEBODY ELSE. JUST--

ALL RIGHT, **ALL RIGHT!** BUT WE'LL CUT IT BACK TO **BIMONTHLY.** OKAY?

THANKS, **STAN.** YOU WON'T BE SORRY.

I SURE **WASN'T**. OVER THE NEXT YEAR AND A HALF, SALES STARTED TO CLIMB AGAIN. SO MUCH SO THAT THE BOOK WENT BACK TO **MONTHLY** WITH ISSUE #20.

AND THEN IT RAN FOR **TWENTY** YEARS.

SO I LEFT THE EDITORSHIP IN **GOOD** HANDS.

AND I TRAVELED, SPREADING THE WORD OF **MARVEL**.

I WENT **EVERYWHERE**.

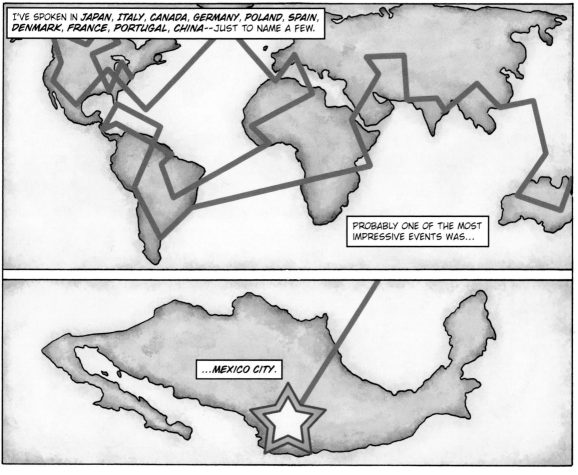

I'VE SPOKEN IN **JAPAN, ITALY, CANADA, GERMANY, POLAND, SPAIN, DENMARK, FRANCE, PORTUGAL, CHINA**--JUST TO NAME A FEW.

PROBABLY ONE OF THE MOST IMPRESSIVE EVENTS WAS...

...*MEXICO CITY*.

DO I REALLY NEED *SIX* BODY-GUARDS?!

YES, SIR, YOU DO.

WHY? I MEAN, DOES *MARVEL* HAVE LOTS OF ENEMIES HERE?

IT'S TO PROTECT YOU FROM THE CROWD.

THE *CROWD*? WHAT'RE YOU EXPECTING THEM TO *DO*?

SOMETIMES THEY'RE TOO ENTHUSIASTIC.

THERE. YOUR FANS AWAIT.

HOLY--!

¡OLÉ! STAN LEE!

MARVEL, MARVEL!

SIGN THIS, POR FAVOR!

I SWEAR, YOU COULD RUN FOR *PRESIDENT* AND YOU'D BE ELECTED RIGHT HERE AND NOW.

I'LL TELL YOU, I HAD FANS IN THE STRANGEST PLACES.

HELLO?

HI, *STAN.* THIS IS PAUL...

PAUL *WHO?*

MCCARTNEY.

I WAS HOPING YOU COULD COME BY THE HOUSE. WANTED TO TALK TO YOU ABOUT SOMETHING.

WAIT... *PAUL MCCARTNEY* THE *BEATLE?*

NOT ANYMORE, BUT *YES.*

CAN YOU COME OVER?

UH... SURE!

SO I WENT.

HE HAD A LIMO OUTSIDE HIS HOUSE THAT LOOKED LIKE IT'D HAD A *BABY BROTHER!*

HOW DID YOU FIND OUT WHERE I WAS STAYING?

OH, I GET BY WITH A LITTLE HELP FROM MY FRIENDS.

SO, *STAN*: MY BAND *WINGS* IS GOING TO BE RELEASING A SONG CALLED "*SEASIDE WOMAN*," WRITTEN AND SUNG BY MY WIFE, *LINDA*.

BUT WE'RE RELEASING IT UNDER A PSEUDONYM: "*SUZY AND THE RED STRIPES*."

"*SUZY*" IS A NAME *LINDA* PICKED UP IN *JAMAICA*. HAS TO DO WITH A GREAT REGGAE VERSION OF "*SUZIE Q*."

SOUNDS GOOD.

AND *RED STRIPE* IS THE MAIN BEER IN *JAMAICA*.

THE POINT IS: WE WANT YOU TO DO A COMIC-BOOK FOR IT.

A *SUZY AND THE RED STRIPES* COMIC? *ABSOLUTELY!* SOUNDS LIKE *FUN!*

BUT YEARS LATER, I RAN INTO HIM AGAIN DURING THE 2014 *SUPER BOWL*. HE'D AGED A BIT. ME, OF COURSE: I LOOKED *EXACTLY THE SAME*.

SO WE SHOOK HANDS ON IT AND WENT OUR SEPARATE WAYS...

BUT THANKS TO *LOUSY* SCHEDULING, OUR PATHS DIDN'T CROSS FOR A WHILE.

AND THEN POOR *LINDA* PASSED AWAY, AND THAT WAS THAT.

PAUL McCARTNEY WAS *NOT* THE MOST OFFBEAT MUSICIAN I EVER ENCOUNTERED.

THAT WOULD BE...

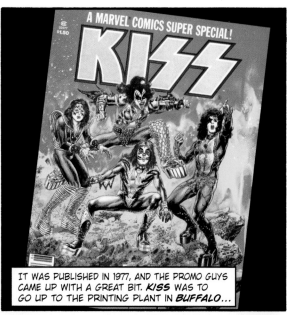

IT WAS PUBLISHED IN 1977, AND THE PROMO GUYS CAME UP WITH A GREAT BIT. *KISS* WAS TO GO UP TO THE PRINTING PLANT IN *BUFFALO*...

...AND THEY WOULD PRICK THEIR FINGER WITH A PIN, AND DRIP A DROP OF THEIR BLOOD INTO THE INK VAT

THAT WAY EVERY *KISS* COMIC WOULD HAVE THE BAND MEMBERS' BLOOD IN IT.

THE GROUP CHARTERED A PLANE TO *BUFFALO* AND I WAS INVITED ALONG. BUT HERE'S WHAT I'LL ALWAYS REMEMBER:

WE HELD UP TRAFFIC LIKE A PRESIDENTIAL MOTORCADE.

ALL I COULD THINK WAS THAT DOCTORS, BUSINESSMEN, AND PARENTS WERE BEING DELAYED SO THAT THESE FOUR GUYS COULD DRIP THEIR *BLOOD* INTO INK...

...SO KIDS WOULD FEEL THEY WERE GETTING REAL *KISS* BLOOD IN THEIR COMICS.

I WASN'T WRITING MUCH AT THAT STAGE.

BUT I STILL SERVED AS A SORT OF *ÉMINENCE GRISE* AROUND THE OFFICES AND HELPED OUT FROM TIME TO TIME.

FOR INSTANCE, THERE WAS A TIME WHEN *GERRY CONWAY*, A VERY TALENTED WRITER WHO HAD TAKEN OVER *AMAZING SPIDER-MAN*, WAS HAVING SOME PROBLEMS.

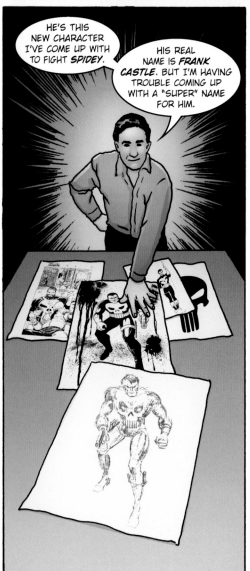

HE'S THIS NEW CHARACTER I'VE COME UP WITH TO FIGHT *SPIDEY*.

HIS REAL NAME IS *FRANK CASTLE*. BUT I'M HAVING TROUBLE COMING UP WITH A "SUPER" NAME FOR HIM.

WHAT DOES HE *DO*? EXACTLY?

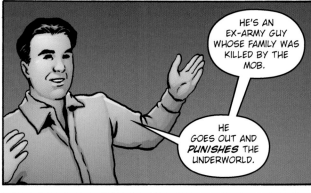

HE'S AN EX-ARMY GUY WHOSE FAMILY WAS KILLED BY THE MOB.

HE GOES OUT AND *PUNISHES* THE UNDERWORLD.

WELL, THERE'S YOUR NAME RIGHT THERE.

Opulent, Sensual, Treacherously Seductive—
Welcome Aboard the World's Most Luxurious
Ocean Liner....

THE Pleasure PALACE

A Novel by

JOAN LEE

DELL • 16950 • **U.S. $3.95**
CAN. $4.95

MEANWHILE, DAUGHTER *JOANIE* GREW UP TO BE A BEAUTIFUL WOMAN CREATING PAINTINGS THAT SHE REFUSED TO SELL, AND DESIGNING JEWELRY THAT SHE *DID* SELL!

SOMETIMES I THINK I'M THE *LEAST CREATIVE* PERSON IN THE FAMILY.

ALTHOUGH I DID ACQUIRE A WRITING JOB I HAVE TO THIS DAY: THE *SPIDER-MAN* NEWSPAPER STRIP.

I WAS APPROACHED BY *DENNY ALLEN*, THE PRESIDENT OF THE *REGISTER AND TRIBUNE* SYNDICATE.

THE AMAZING SPIDER-MAN

STAN LEE

POSSESSING INCREDIBLE "SPIDER-POWERS", PETER PARKER USES HIS SCIENTIFIC WIZARDRY TO CREATE AN ARTIFICIAL WEB-SHOOTER---

THWIP!

--A SIMPLE DEVICE, MAKING HIM MASTER OF THE CITY'S ROOF TOPS!

HE SAID I COULD HAVE A FREE HAND TO DO A DAILY STRIP HOWEVER I WANTED.

WOW!

I SAID, "WOW!"

OUCH! WHAT'S WITH THE ELBOW, HONEY?

I DECIDED TO PLAY UP THE *SOAP OPERA* ASPECTS, ALTHOUGH I DID MANAGE TO DROP IN COLORFUL VILLAINS. AND IT SEEMED TO WORK.

AND I ALSO OPTED TO KEEP *SPIDER-MAN* AND *MARY JANE* MARRIED, DESPITE THE STORY LINE THAT...

WHICH IT JUST MIGHT!

OH. DID I FORGET TO MENTION?

THINGS WENT DOWNHILL FROM THERE, ESPECIALLY WHEN THEY TRIED TO USE THE *HULK* TO SPRINGBOARD OTHER *MARVEL* HEROES.

UNFORTUNATELY THE NETWORKS WENT TO TOWN ON THEM WITH WHAT THEY WEREN'T ALLOWED TO DO.

TAKE *THOR*, FOR INSTANCE.

THE NETWORK DECLARED THAT AMERICA WOULDN'T ACCEPT THE NOTION OF A GOD WHO WASN'T *THE* GOD.

AN OBJECTION THAT *NO ONE* HAD RAISED DURING *TWENTY YEARS* OF THE COMICS.

SO *THOR* BECAME A REINCARNATED *VIKING WARRIOR*.

THAT WENT OVER WELL.

THAT WASN'T *HALF* AS BAD AS WHAT THEY DID WITH *DAREDEVIL*, THOUGH.

ONCE AGAIN AN OBJECTION RULED THE DAY: NO HORNS.

THEY DIDN'T WANT HIM TO LOOK *SATANIC*.

HIS COSTUME WENT FROM RED TO BLACK AND, BEST OF ALL, THEY PUT A BLINDFOLD ON HIM.

BECAUSE HE'S *BLIND*.

I POINTED OUT THAT THIS WAS *RIDICULOUS* BECAUSE IT ADVERTISED HIS GREATEST SECRET, BUT THEY DIDN'T CARE.

BUT AT LEAST WE CAN FEEL GOOD ABOUT *MARVEL'S AGENTS OF S.H.I.E.L.D.* AND *AGENT CARTER*!

BE HAPPY WITH WHAT YOU'VE GOT!

THANK YOU ALL FOR COMING. SO HERE'S THE THING:

AS YOU KNOW, WE'RE MAKING INROADS INTO ANIMATION. BUT WE NEED TO RUN OUR OWN STUDIO TO GET IT DONE RIGHT.

WE DON'T NEED THE CARTOON EQUIVALENT OF THE LIVE-ACTION *SPIDEY* OR *DAREDEVIL*.

AFTER GIVING IT A *GOOD DEAL* OF THOUGHT, I'VE DECIDED THAT I'M *WILLING* TO UPROOT MYSELF AND MY FAMILY AND MOVE TO LOS ANGELES...

...FOR *MARVEL*.

THERE I WILL SET UP AN ANIMATION STUDIO FOR THE COMPANY AND RUN IT.

I HAVE EVERY CONFIDENCE THAT *JIM SHOOTER* HERE WILL BE ABLE TO KEEP A SOLID HAND ON THE BULLPEN.

AND THAT YOU WILL *ALL* CONTINUE TO TURN OUT THE QUALITY OF *MARVEL COMICS* THAT EVERY-ONE HAS COME TO EXPECT!

HUZZAH!

HUZZAH!

DID THEY BUY IT?

ONE *HUNDRED* PERCENT!

WE'RE MOVING TO L.A., GUYS!

AWRIGHT!!

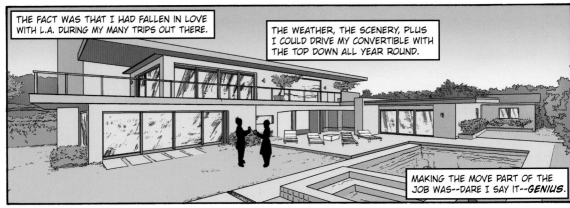

THE FACT WAS THAT I HAD FALLEN IN LOVE WITH L.A. DURING MY MANY TRIPS OUT THERE.

THE WEATHER, THE SCENERY, PLUS I COULD DRIVE MY CONVERTIBLE WITH THE TOP DOWN ALL YEAR ROUND.

MAKING THE MOVE PART OF THE JOB WAS--DARE I SAY IT--*GENIUS*.

TO OUR *NEW LIVES!*

UH, *STAN*...DO YOU *HEAR* SOMETHING?

LIKE...*MUSIC?* COMING FROM THE GUESTHOUSE?

YOU'RE RIGHT. YOU THINK IT'S SOMETHING THE PREVIOUS OWNER LEFT FOR US?

WHY WOULD THERE BE MUSIC PLAYING?

I HAVEN'T THE FAINTEST ID--

WHAT THE--?!

HI. YOU MUST BE MY NEW LANDLORDS.

BELIEVE IT OR NOT, THE PREVIOUS OWNER HAD RENTED THE GUESTHOUSE TO SOMEONE AND NEVER TOLD US.

WE HAD TO BRING IN A LAWYER AND THREATEN THE REAL ESTATE AGENT BEFORE WE COULD GET RID OF HIM.

SO THAT WAS FUN.

WE SET UP OUR STUDIO IN A PERFECT ONE-STORY BUILDING IN VAN NUYS.

I FILLED IT WITH VIDEOTAPES OF MY INTERVIEWS AND LECTURES OVER THE YEARS.

AND A *BEAUTIFUL* BUST OF *JOANIE* THAT HAD BEEN SCULPTED YEARS AGO BY A FRIEND NAMED *STANLEY SAWYER*.

AND *THEN* ONE NIGHT...

YES, THIS IS *STAN LEE*. HOW CAN I HELP Y--

WHAT?!

THE FIRE DEPARTMENT SUSPECTED *ARSON*, ALTHOUGH THEY NEVER FOUND THE ARSONIST.

I LOST EVERY TAPE AND, OF COURSE, THE BEAUTIFUL BUST OF *JOANIE*.

BUT AT LEAST NO ONE WAS HURT.

AND I CAN'T SAY THAT MY INITIAL MEETING WITH A NETWORK EXECUTIVE WENT THAT MUCH BETTER.

SO TELL ME, *MR. LEE*: WHAT DO YOU THINK OF OUR SATURDAY MORNING CARTOONS?

WELL, THEY'RE *BEAUTIFULLY* ANIMATED. BUT THE STORIES ARE LARGELY *UNINTELLIGENT*.

THE CHARACTERS SPEAK IN CARTOON SPEAK INSTEAD OF REAL DIALOGUE.

WE DON'T WANT OUR SERIES TO CONSIST OF TALKING HEADS.

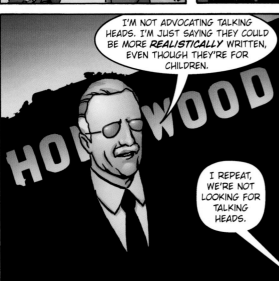

I'M NOT ADVOCATING TALKING HEADS. I'M JUST SAYING THEY COULD BE MORE *REALISTICALLY* WRITTEN, EVEN THOUGH THEY'RE FOR CHILDREN.

I REPEAT, WE'RE NOT LOOKING FOR TALKING HEADS.

ALL I'M SUGGESTING IS *BETTER* DIALOGUE THAT COULD--

WE'RE NOT LOOKING FOR TALKING HEADS.

IT WAS LIKE THE *MAD TEA PARTY*. THAT'S *ALL* SHE KEPT REPEATING.

Welcome to Hollywood.

IN THE MEANTIME, THINGS WERE CHANGING WITH **MARVEL** YET AGAIN.

CADENCE INDUSTRIES

CADENCE SOLD **MARVEL COMICS** AND WE HAD A NEW OWNER.

I'D BEEN THROUGH THIS ENOUGH TIMES THAT I WAS PRETTY INURED TO IT.

NEW WORLD

BUT I WAS EAGER TO SEE WHAT WAS GOING TO HAPPEN NOW THAT WE WERE A **NEW WORLD** COMPANY.

FINALLY THE DAY CAME. ONE BY ONE THE VARIOUS **MARVEL** EXECS WERE USHERED INTO THE LION'S DEN.

AND THEN IT WAS **MY** TURN.

HUGE FAN!

ME **FIRST!**

CAN YOU SIGN THIS?

SOOO **THAT** WORKED OUT OKAY.

AND THAT WAS IT! EVERYTHING WORKED OUT FINE AND *NEW WORLD* OWNS *MARVEL* TO THIS DAY.

NEW WORLD

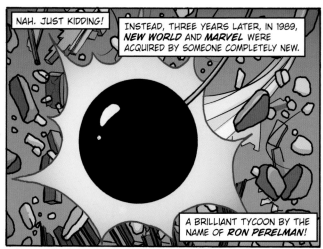

NAH. JUST KIDDING!

INSTEAD, THREE YEARS LATER, IN 1989, *NEW WORLD* AND *MARVEL* WERE ACQUIRED BY SOMEONE COMPLETELY NEW.

A BRILLIANT TYCOON BY THE NAME OF *RON PERELMAN*!

NO, NOT *THAT* GUY!

THAT'S *"PERLMAN"*!

PERELMAN, WITH AN EXTRA *"E"*!

I WAS EXCITED THAT *MARVEL* WAS FINALLY BEING TAKEN OVER BY A BRILLIANT MAN WHO HEADED A VERY WEALTHY CONGLOMERATE.

I WAS TO HAVE A MEETING WITH A GENT NAMED *BILL BEVINS*, WHO WAS GOING TO BE RUNNING THE COMPANY FOR *RON*.

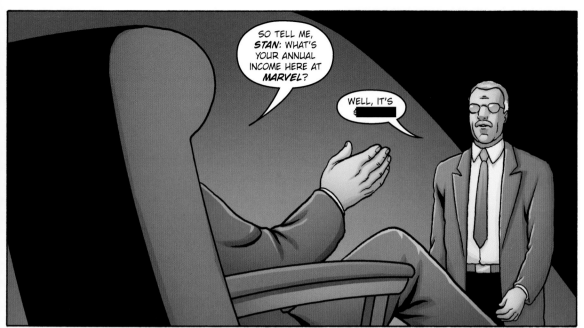

SO TELL ME, *STAN*: WHAT'S YOUR ANNUAL INCOME HERE AT *MARVEL*?

WELL, IT'S $▮▮▮▮▮

HMMM.

OKAY, WELL, FROM NOW ON, YOU'RE GOING TO BE EARNING DOUBLE THAT.

AH-OOOOO-GAH

I'M SORRY. *WHAT?* DID YOU *SAY*--

DOUBLE, YES.

WOW. I WONDER WHAT *JOANIE* WILL SAY WHEN SHE SEES MY NEXT CHECK.

ANYTHING GOOD IN THE MAIL, HONEY?

AH-OOOOO-GAH

BY THE WAY, THIS IS MY DESK. I WORK ON A COMPUTER THESE DAYS.

I USED TO WORK ON ONE OF THESE.

IT'S CALLED A "TYPEWRITER." CHANCES ARE, MANY OF YOU READING THIS HAVE NEVER EVEN SEEN ONE, MUCH LESS USED IT.

BUT ONLY A FEW DECADES AGO, I SAT AT THIS AND TYPED ONTO ACTUAL PAPER.

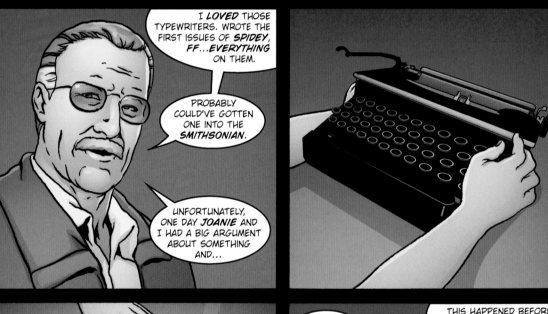

I LOVED THOSE TYPEWRITERS. WROTE THE FIRST ISSUES OF SPIDEY, FF...EVERYTHING ON THEM.

PROBABLY COULD'VE GOTTEN ONE INTO THE SMITHSONIAN.

UNFORTUNATELY, ONE DAY JOANIE AND I HAD A BIG ARGUMENT ABOUT SOMETHING AND...

WAAAM

* SIGH *

THIS HAPPENED BEFORE EBAY. TOO BAD. I COULD'VE AUCTIONED THE PARTS AND MADE A MINT.

Annnnyway...

COMICS SALES WERE GOING GREAT.

NEWSPAPERS KEPT WRITING ABOUT WHAT GREAT INVESTMENTS COMICS WERE, AND PEOPLE STARTED TAKING THAT SERIOUSLY.

SO INSTEAD OF A READER BUYING ONLY THE COMICS HE WANTED...

...HE STARTED BUYING SOME *EXTRAS*...

...AND THEN A *LOT* OF EXTRAS. AND THEN...

WELL, YOU GET THE IDEA.

THE COLLECTORS FIGURED THIS WAS WHEN THEY WERE GOING TO MAKE THE **BIG PROFITS** WITH THEIR PURCHASES.

SO THEY HEADED TO THEIR LOCAL COMICBOOK STORES...

...ONLY TO DISCOVER THERE WAS ONLY A SPECIAL, **LIMITED** MARKET FOR THEM.

ONLY BUYING GOLDEN AGE COMICS!

ONLY BUYING GOLDEN AGE COMICS!

OLD COMICS WERE VALUABLE BECAUSE THEY WERE **RARE**. BUT PUBLISHERS HAD BEEN PRODUCING **MILLIONS** OF COPIES OF NEW TITLES.

THE ANGRY COLLECTORS PULLED OUT OF THE HOBBY ENTIRELY...

...AND RETAILERS SOON FOLLOWED. WE WENT FROM WHERE THERE WERE ONCE OVER SIX THOUSAND STORES TO WHERE THERE WERE NOW ONLY TWO THOUSAND.

CLOSED FOR GOOD

AND THE PUBLISHERS TOOK A MAJOR HIT AS WELL. THE ENTIRE MARKETPLACE WAS **COLLAPSING**.

AT THAT POINT, **MARVEL** RAN INTO SOME MAJOR DIFFICULTIES. FINANCIAL PROBLEMS WITH ANOTHER DIVISION, **FLEER BASEBALL CARDS,** SENT THE COMPANY INTO SUCH A DOWNWARD SPIRAL...

...THAT A FAMED CORPORATE RAIDER SET HIS SIGHTS ON **MARVEL**.

CARL ICAHN. EVERONE WOUND UP LOCKED IN CORPORATE MANEUVERS THAT COMPELLED THE COMPANY TO FILE FOR CHAPTER 11 BANKRUPTCY FOR **MARVEL**.

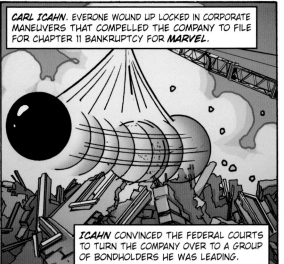

ICAHN CONVINCED THE FEDERAL COURTS TO TURN THE COMPANY OVER TO A GROUP OF BONDHOLDERS HE WAS LEADING.

BUT THEN SOMETHING REALLY **UNEXPECTED** HAPPENED.

ANOTHER COMPANY, **TOY BIZ**, RUN BY **AVI ARAD** AND **IKE PERLMUTTER**, ENTERED THE PICTURE.

SOMEHOW, IN 1997, **AVI** AND **IKE** MANAGED TO SNATCH **MARVEL** AWAY, AND THE BANKS SIDED WITH THEM.

ME, I WAS FOLLOWING THIS FROM THE OUTSIDE LOOKING IN.

EXCUSE ME!

IT'S OUT THE SIDE DOOR, DOWN THE HALL, ON THE LEFT.

NO, THAT'S NOT WHAT I...

I WAS JUST WONDERING HOW YOU DO IT.

HOW YOU WRITE.

I WANNA BE A WRITER SOME- DAY AND I WAS HOPING MAYBE YOU COULD GIVE ME SOME *POINTERS.*

SURE COULD.

AND *HAVE.*

HERE'S A WHOLE *BOOK* ON IT!

STAN LEE'S HOW TO WRITE COMICS

THANKS!

WHOA!! CAN *I* HAVE A COPY?!

UH, *SORRY,* GUYS! JUST HAD THE *ONE*! BUT EVERYONE *CALM DOWN*!

IF IT'LL HELP, I'LL GIVE YOU SOME HANDY BITS OF ADVICE THAT I ALWAYS FOLLOW TO GUIDE YOU ON YOUR WAYS!

AND DON'T GET *DISCOURAGED!* LOTS OF *REALLY GOOD,* SUCCESSFUL WRITERS DIDN'T MAKE THEIR FIRST SALE UNTIL LONG AFTER THEY STARTED WRITING.

OF COURSE, IF YOU'VE BEEN UNABLE TO SELL ANYTHING FOR YEARS AND YEARS AND ARE NOW *STARVING AND HOMELESS,* YOU MIGHT START THINKING OF *ANOTHER* VOCATION.

BUT SHORT OF THAT, STAY WITH IT. *TOMORROW MAY BE YOUR LUCKY DAY!*

NOW... WHERE WAS I?

OH, *RIGHT!* BACK TO *ME!*

SO THE *"NEW" MARVEL* WOUND UP GIVING ME A *LIFETIME* CONTRACT AND A FAIR SALARY, AND THE TITLE *"CHAIRMAN EMERITUS."*

I ALSO MET SOME INTERESTING PEOPLE AROUND THEN. FOR INSTANCE...

PLEASURE TO MEET YOU, *MR. PRESIDENT.*

YOU TOO, *STAN.* AND THIS LOVELY LADY IS...?

I COULDN'T RESIST SAYING...

THIS IS MY TROPHY WIFE, *JOAN.*

HERE'S THE KICKER. A FEW WEEKS LATER, AT A FUND-RAISING COCKTAIL PARTY, WE RAN INTO *HILLARY CLINTON* AGAIN.

I WASN'T SURE SHE'D REMEMBER ME, SO...

HELLO, *MRS. CLINTON.* YOU PROBABLY DON'T REMEMBER, BUT I'M...

HELLO, *STAN!* HOW ARE YOU AND YOUR TROPHY WIFE?

SHE SURE DID REMEMBER!

ALSO AROUND THEN I WAS TALKED INTO STARTING UP AN *INTERNET* COMPANY. SEEMED LIKE A GOOD IDEA AT THE TIME.

It wasn't.

It ended badly and the less said the better.

I ALSO MET A GREAT EXECUTIVE NAMED *GILL CHAMPION*. AND TOGETHER WE CAME UP WITH A *NEW* COMPANY:

PURVEYORS OF WONDER, OR *POW! ENTERTAINMENT*, FOR SHORT!

Stan Lee's

POW!

ENTERTAINMENT

I WAS FINALLY ABLE TO COME UP WITH MY OWN CHARACTERS AND, BEST OF ALL, HOLD ON TO THE RIGHTS FOR THEM!

SOMETHING THAT HADN'T BEEN AN OPTION WHILE WORKING FOR *MARVEL*.

LET'S SEE IF YOU REMEMBER ONE OF MY EARLIEST *POW!* CREATIONS.

IN CASE YOU DON'T RECALL, LET ME GIVE YOU A *TOTALLY NEUTRAL* PICTURE TO JOG YOUR MEMORY:

YOU JOGGED YET?

ANYWAY, WE SOLD THE ANIMATED SERIES TO THE NEWLY CREATED *SPIKE TV*. IT WAS CALLED...

I'M ALSO WORKING WITH CREATORS AROUND THE WORLD, COMING UP WITH CHARACTERS THAT REFLECT THEIR *CULTURES*.

THESE INCLUDE *ULTIMO*, FROM JAPAN...

KARAKURIDÔJI **ULTIMO**

STAN LEE ✕ HIROYUKI TAKEI

STAN LEE AND YOSHIKI'S
BLOOD RED DRAGON
#0

...*BLOOD RED DRAGON*, ALSO JAPANESE, WHICH WILL STAR MUSIC SUPERSTAR *YOSHIKI*...

...AND, FROM *INDIA*, *CHAKRA*, THE *INVINCIBLE!*

Stan Lee's
CHAKRA
THE INVINCIBLE

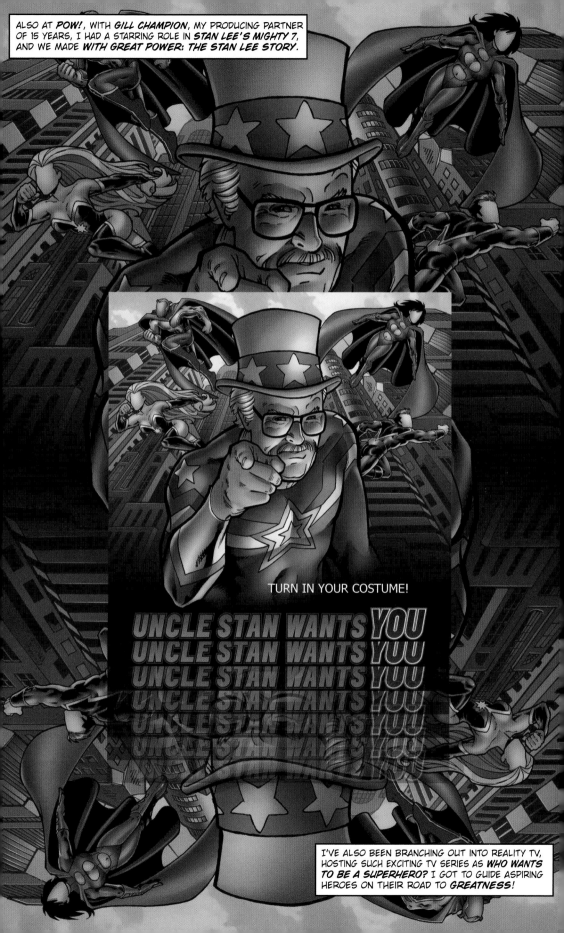

MEANWHILE, AS THAT WAS GOING ON, *MARVEL* WAS STILL *STRUGGLING* TO GET THEATRICAL FILMS UP AND RUNNING. THE BATTLE HAD BEEN GOING ON FOR *YEARS.*

THERE WAS A *CAPTAIN AMERICA* FILM IN 1990 THAT WASN'T EVEN ABLE TO GET RELEASED FOR TWO YEARS.

THE *RED SKULL* WAS *ITALIAN!* WHAT THE *HELL?*

BUT AT LEAST IT GOT *SOME* RELEASE. THE 1994 VERSION OF THE *FANTASTIC FOUR* WAS SO *BAD* THAT IT WAS *NEVER* DISTRIBUTED.

SOME CLAIM IT WAS ONLY MADE FOR LEGAL REASONS, FOR THE STUDIO TO HOLD ON TO THE RIGHTS.

MEANWHILE, THE *MICHAEL KEATON/ TIM BURTON BATMAN* WAS RAKING IN *HUNDREDS OF MILLIONS.* IT WAS *AGGRAVATING,* TO BE SURE.

ONE DAY IN 1993, I GOT A PACKAGE FROM *CAROLCO*, THEN CURRENT OWNERS OF THE RIGHTS TO MAKE A *SPIDER-MAN* MOVIE.

I WAS IN PUPPY HEAVEN BECAUSE OF THE CONTENTS.

A FIFTY-SEVEN-PAGE TREATMENT FOR A *SPIDEY* MOVIE BY NONE OTHER THAN *JIM CAMERON*, CREATOR OF *THE TERMINATOR*.

SPIDER-MAN

TREATMENT
BY
JAMES CAMERON

EYES ONLY:
NOT FOR DUPLICATION

AS I GREEDILY PORED OVER PAGE AFTER PAGE, I COULD SEE EACH SCENE UNFOLDING IN MY IMAGINATION.

WE'RE THERE.

UNFORTUNATELY, WE *WEREN'T*.

THE ENTIRE THING DEVOLVED INTO A HUGE LEGAL MESS DEALING WITH THE RIGHT TO PRODUCE *SPIDER-MAN* THAT I DON'T LIKE TO THINK ABOUT BECAUSE IT GIVES ME A *HEADACHE*.

FOR NEARLY TWO YEARS AFTER THAT, LAWYERS MET AND ARGUED AND SUED AND COUNTERSUED.

IT WAS LIKE A MASSIVE SINKING SHIP.

WHO KNOWS? MAYBE THAT'S WHERE *JIM CAMERON* GOT THE IDEA FOR HIS NEXT MOVIE.

EVENTUALLY, AFTER ALL THE BACK-AND-FORTH AND *MILLIONS* OF LEGAL FEES SPENT...

...THEY FINALLY WORKED EVERYTHING OUT.

AND THEY BROUGHT IN A GREAT DIRECTOR, *SAM RAIMI*.

AND SAM, IN TURN, DIRECTED THIS:

...THIS GUY!

IT WAS A PRETTY BRIEF APPEARANCE. RIGHT WHEN THE GREEN GOBLIN IS SMASHING THINGS UP...

...I RUN IN AND SAVE A LITTLE GIRL FROM A PIECE OF FALLING RUBBLE.

YES, IN ONE OF MY EARLIEST APPEARANCES, I WAS A HERO.

THANK YOU ALL.

ACTUALLY, OVER THE YEARS, AS MARVEL MOVED INTO THE FILM INDUSTRY AND OTHER STUDIOS ALSO OPTIONED OUR HEROES...

...MY CAMEOS HAVE BECOME ALMOST TRADITION! ALFRED HITCHCOCK HAS NOTHING ON ME!

ONE OF MY FAVORITES IS FROM FANTASTIC FOUR: RISE OF THE SILVER SURFER, MOSTLY BECAUSE IT'S BASED ON AN ACTUAL COMIC CAMEO!

SEE, WAAAAY BACK IN FANTASTIC FOUR ANNUAL #3, JACK KIRBY AND I WERE KEPT OUT OF REED AND SUE'S WEDDING.

YOU HEARD THE MAN, GENTS! NOW YA BETTER GO PEACEABLE!

BUT YOU CAN'T KEEP US OUT!

DON'T BET ON IT, MISTER!

THIS WAY OUT, YOU GUYS!

YOU HAVEN'T HEARD THE LAST OF THIS! WE HAVE WAYS OF GETTING EVEN!

BEAT IT, YA BUMS! I BEEN THREATENED BY EXPERTS!

AW, GO GARGLE A GRENADE, YA BIG STIFF!

HOW ABOUT THAT?? IMAGINE THEM KEEPIN' US OUT, STAN!

WE'LL SHOW 'EM, JACK! LET'S GET BACK TO THE BULLPEN AND START WRITING THE NEXT ISH!

THE END

AND THERE YOU HAVE IT! SUE AND REED ARE NOW MAN AND WIFE--AND WE HOPE YOU GOT A FEW CHUCKLES, AND A FEW THRILLS OUT OF OUR TALE! A NEW CHAPTER IN THE LIFE OF THE F.F. WILL SOON BEGIN, AND WE'LL SHARE IT WITH YOU TOGETHER ...AS ALWAYS!

23

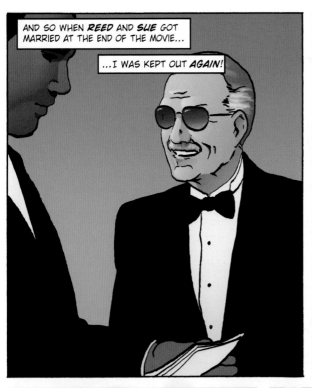

AND SO WHEN *REED* AND *SUE* GOT MARRIED AT THE END OF THE MOVIE...

...I WAS KEPT OUT *AGAIN*!

WHICH IS WEIRD, CONSIDERING I WAS *WILLIE LUMPKIN* IN THE PREVIOUS *FF* MOVIE! YOU'D THINK THEY'D HAVE LET THEIR FAITHFUL *MAILMAN* IN!

I LOVE DOING CAMEOS. ANOTHER FAVORITE OF MINE IS FROM THE FIRST *IRON MAN* MOVIE.

HEY, *HEF*. GOOD TO SEE YOU.

BUT MY ABSOLUTE FAVORITE, SO FAR, IS THE NEW *AVENGERS: AGE OF ULTRON*.

AS OF THIS WRITING, IT HASN'T COME OUT YET, SO I DON'T KNOW HOW MUCH, IF ANY, WILL BE IN IT.

SO HERE'S THE WHOLE THING, TO THE BEST OF MY RECOLLECTION.

IRONICALLY, MY CAMEOS WOUND UP ELEVATING MY CAREER AGAIN!

IT BECAME TRADITION TO SEE **STAN THE MAN** WANDERING THROUGH **MARVEL** PRODUCTIONS.

SO MUCH SO THAT I WOUND UP IN OTHER THINGS OUTSIDE OF **MARVEL**!

I ACTUALLY HAD A SUPPORTING ROLE IN THE GREAT **KEVIN SMITH**'S WILD FILM **MALLRATS**. WITH A BEARD, NO LESS!

I HIT ON **JULIE ANDREWS** IN **THE PRINCESS DIARIES**.

HECK, I EVEN HAD A GUEST ROLE IN THE MOST **POPULAR** SITCOM ON THE AIR.

NAMELY, **THE BIG BANG THEORY**, WHERE I WOUND UP BEING YET ANOTHER BIG SHOT WHOM **SHELDON COOPER** HARASSED.

I'VE ACTUALLY HAD TINY ROLES IN **DOZENS** OF MOVIES AND TELEVISION PROGRAMS.

NOT BAD FOR A **WRITER**, HUH?

THEN ONE DAY I GOT A CALL...

STAN? MICHAEL USLAN.

MICHAEL! **GREAT** TO HEAR FROM YOU! I HEAR PRODUCING THE **BATMAN** FILMS HAS GONE VERY WELL FOR YOU.

YEAH, YOU COULD SAY THAT.

LOOK, **STAN:** WORD'S OUT THAT YOU'RE NOW FREE TO WRITE WHATEVER YOU WANT FOR WHOMEVER YOU WANT.

RIGHT.

HOW'D YOU LIKE TO WRITE A SERIES FOR **DC**?

STAN?

YOU'VE **GOTTA** BE KIDDING!

WHA--? HOW'D YOU GET HERE THAT *QUICK*?!

MY CAR'S PRETTY FAST. YOU DONE LAUGHING YET?

MICHAEL, I'VE BEEN ASSOCIATED WITH *MARVEL* SINCE DINOSAURS WALKED THE EARTH.

THERE'S NO WAY THAT *DC*, OUR BIGGEST COMPETITOR, WOULD HAVE ME WRITE FOR ANY OF THEIR MAGS.

NO, NO. IT WOULD BE YOUR OWN MAGAZINE.

WHAT I'D WANT IS FOR YOU TO TAKE *DC'S* TWELVE TOP CHARACTERS AND WRITE THEM AS IF *YOU YOURSELF* CREATED THEM.

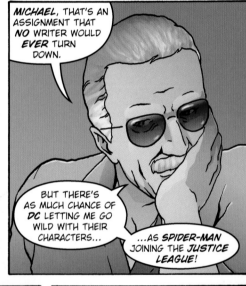

MICHAEL, THAT'S AN ASSIGNMENT THAT *NO* WRITER WOULD *EVER* TURN DOWN.

BUT THERE'S AS MUCH CHANCE OF *DC* LETTING ME GO WILD WITH THEIR CHARACTERS...

...AS *SPIDER-MAN* JOINING THE *JUSTICE LEAGUE*!

NO HARM IN ASKING. I'LL LET YOU KNOW.

I FIGURED THAT WAS THAT.

EXCEPT, A WEEK LATER...

STAN? *MICHAEL!* WE *HAVE* A DEAL!

HUH?

IT'S GOING TO BE CALLED, *"JUST IMAGINE IF STAN LEE CREATED--!"*

CRIPES! NOW WHAT? I MEAN, HOW WILL THE FANS REACT IF, I DUNNO...

...IF *SUPERMAN* WAS THE *WEAKEST* MEMBER OF THE KRYPTONIAN POLICE FORCE...

...OR IF **AQUAMAN** WAS ACTUALLY A CHARACTER MADE OUT OF WATER...

...WHICH WAS, BY THE WAY, A STORY LINE THEY EVENTUALLY ACTUALLY DID IN THE COMICS LINE ITSELF. GO FIGURE!

BUT I DID IT, WRITING THOSE TWO AND TEN OTHERS. AND THE FANS HAVEN'T BURNED ME IN EFFIGY, AT LEAST AS FAR AS I KNOW.

MAN, WHAT AN EXCITING LIFE I'VE LEAD. HARD TO BELIEVE, CONSIDERING HOW I STARTED OUT.

I EVEN GOT MY OWN ACTION FIGURE. IN 2007, *MARVEL* INTRODUCED A *STAN LEE* ACTION FIGURE. THE BODY BENEATH THE FIGURE'S CLOTHES WAS AN ACTUAL MOLD OF A *SPIDER-MAN* ACTION FIGURE.

I'VE ALSO BEEN BLESSED TO MEET MANY PEOPLE. LIKE, OH...

GEORGE W. BUSH.

HE WAS GIVING OUT THE *NATIONAL MEDAL OF ARTS* TO ME AND THE WONDERFUL *OLIVIA De HAVILLAND.*

SO *BUSH* GAVE HER THE MEDAL.

AND THEN HE KISSED HER ON THE CHEEK.

THEN IT WAS MY TURN, AND I SAID THE FIRST THING THAT OCCURRED TO ME.

YOU'RE NOT GONNA KISS *ME,* ARE YOU?

AND HE JUST BROKE UP. THE OFFICIAL PICTURE THAT WAS TAKEN WAS OF THE PREZ AND ME LAUGHING OUT LOUD.

THERE WAS ONE TIME I WAS AT *CNN* FOR AN INTERVIEW. I WAS THERE WITH MY EVENT COORDINATOR, *MAX ANDERSON*.

HEY, *STAN!*

HI!

Y'KNOW, YOU LOOK JUST LIKE *GEORGE CLOONEY.*

YEAH, I GET TOLD THAT A LOT.

KNOW SOMETHING, *STAN?*

WHAT?

THAT *WAS* GEORGE CLOONEY.

I RAN INTO HIM LATER AND TOLD HIM SOMETIMES I DON'T SEE TOO WELL.

AND HE SAID HE WISHED *MORE* PEOPLE WOULDN'T RECOGNIZE HIM. COOL, HUH?

AND THERE WAS AN AWARDS SHOW I ONCE ATTENDED. I WAS THERE WITH MY BEAUTIFUL *JOAN* ON MY ARM.

LATER I RAN INTO *BRAD PITT* AND I TOLD HIM NOT TO WORRY. I WON'T TRY OUT FOR ANY OF HIS ROLES.

HE LOOKED KINDA GRATEFUL.

AND THEN I MET *STEVEN SPIELBERG*.

I TOLD HIM THAT I WANTED TO WRITE SOME NEW STORIES FOR HIM AND GIVE HIM SOME TIPS ON DIRECTING.

THANK HEAVENS HE HAS A SENSE OF *HUMOR*.

AND HERE ARE MY DAUGHTER *J.C.* AND ME AT THE PREMIERE OF *THOR 2* WITH *ANTHONY HOPKINS*.

I LOVE BRINGING *J.C.* TO PREMIERES.

AND I LIKE THE FACT THAT SHE LOOKS AS GLAMOROUS AS ANY OF THE STARS.

BUT YOU KNOW WHAT? AT THE END OF THE DAY, IT'S NOT REALLY ABOUT THE FAMOUS PEOPLE.

IT'S ABOUT YOU GUYS.

THE FANS.

I WANT TO KEEP SEEING YOU AND HEARING WHAT YOU'VE GOT TO SAY. AND NOW WE EVEN HAVE OUR OWN CONVENTION: *STAN LEE'S COMIKAZE!*

BUT STILL, IT'S THE *UNEXPECTED* MEETINGS THAT...

LEMME GIVE YOU AN EXAMPLE.

I WAS AT *UNIVERSAL STUDIOS* IN *FLORIDA.* ONE OF THE VICE PRESIDENTS WANTED TO GIVE ME A PERSONAL TOUR, BUT I JUST DECIDED TO WALK AROUND.

AND NOBODY NOTICED ME.

IT WAS KIND OF DEPRESSING. THAT WAS, UNTIL I GOT TO *STAN LEE BOULEVARD.*

THEN I GOT SPOTTED, AND I WAS SURROUNDED BY AUTOGRAPH SEEKERS.

IT WAS *GREAT!* THEN...

WHOAAAA! SLOW DOWN, FELLA! YOU OKAY?

HE'S SUCH A HUGE FAN OF YOURS. ALWAYS HAS BEEN.

More than a fan.

MY FATHER DIED WHEN I WAS A KID. AND FOR THE LONGEST TIME, I WAS SO SAD NOT HAVING A DAD.

YEAH, BUT THEN MY MOTHER BOUGHT ME AMAZING SPIDER-MAN.

I'M SO SORRY.

I KNOW THAT MOST COMICS ARE JUST FOR FUN, BUT PETER PARKER SPOKE TO ME...

...AND HE WAS DOING SO MUCH WITH HIS LIFE THAT WAS... WELL... AMAZING.

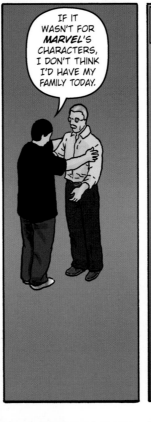

IF IT WASN'T FOR MARVEL'S CHARACTERS, I DON'T THINK I'D HAVE MY FAMILY TODAY.

I KNOW, I KNOW...THAT MAY SOUND SELF-AGGRANDIZING. BUT IT'S NOT MEANT TO BE.

I WAS JUST SO TOUCHED TO REALIZE THAT IN A LIFETIME OF MAKING UP STORIES ABOUT SUPERHEROES...YOU CAN TRULY CONNECT WITH PEOPLE.

THAT YOU CAN OFFER A HAND...

...TO SOMEBODY IN NEED OF A LIFT.

EXCUSE ME.

OH! IT'S *YOU*! WHAT'S UP, KID?

COULD YOU TELL ME ALL ABOUT *JOANIE* AGAIN? SHE SOUNDS *WONDERFUL*.

ABSOLUTELY.

EVERYTHING YOU WANNA KNOW. ALTHOUGH I'LL START OFF WITH *THIS*:

COMICS, ANIMATION, SHOWBIZ... MAYBE I DID OKAY, MAYBE NOT.

BUT IF SHE'S *STILL* SMILING AFTER NEARLY *SIX DECADES* OF MARRIAGE...

...THAT'S *ALL* THAT REALLY MATTERS.

C'MON, KID, I'LL GET YOU A MILKSHAKE.

**SIMON &
SCHUSTER**

Simon & Schuster UK Ltd
1st Floor
222 Gray's Inn Road
London WC1X 8HB

First published in Great Britain by Simon & Schuster UK Ltd, 2015
A CBS company

Text copyright © 2015 by POW! Entertainment

Art copyright © 2015 by Colleen Doran

All Marvel Comics art and related characters © Marvel

"Just Imagine Stan Lee's Superman" and "Just Imagine Stan Lee's Aquaman" copyright DC Comics

Soldier Zero, Starborn, and Traveler are copyright 2011-2015 Boom Entertainment and POW! Entertainment

Chakra, the Invincible © 2015 Graphic India Pte. Ltd. and POW! Entertainment. Artwork by Graphic India Pte. Ltd.

Heroman © B, P, W / HPC / TX

Blood Red Dragon © 2015 Sky Entertainment and POW! Entertainment

This book is copyright under the Berne Convention.
No reproduction without permission.
All rights reserved.

www.simonandschuster.co.uk

Simon & Schuster Australia,
Sydney

Simon & Schuster India,
New Delhi

A CIP catalogue record for this book is available from the British Library

Paperback ISBN: 978-1-4711-5259-7
Ebook ISBN: 978-1-4711-5260-3

Manufactured in the United States of America